EARLY PRAISE FOR TERROR AT THE SOUND OF A WHISTLE

Caroline has worked for many years on *Terror at the Sound of a Whistle*, painstakingly peeling back multifaceted layers of a long-buried childhood trauma. As she allows her inner child to reintroduce her to the depth of the pain she tucked away, to move on as she thought one should, she finds that young Caroline along with the sound of a whistle have other plans, casting doubt on choices made, roads not taken... and a road that suddenly closed.

— WALTER RABCHUK, M.A. ED,
EDUCATION CONSULTANT

Caroline Shannon Davenport creates a world where little things matter, where a kind word can change lives. Her characters' strong moral compasses point true north and guide them to establish priorities that help them navigate an ever-changing world. I only wish that Davenport had been around when I worked at Curtis Brown Literary Agency.

— WENDY FRENCH, AUTHOR OF
SMOTHERING, GOING COASTAL, AND
AFTER THE RICE

T0120401

Caroline's novel is a finely-crafted remembrance of first love that takes us back on a journey to a time and place long gone and forever changed, but not forgotten. She teases out memories almost faded like a morning dream and brings them to life for us. Did such people exist, really? Was there ever such a time? Indeed, there was.

A coming-of-age story in a now almost bygone time, the 1950s through the early 60s. The author calls this a "novelistic memoir," but her true story is powerful and captivating enough to have been a towering fiction, or maybe that's the way real life really is when told by a pro. Chocked full of memorable detail, delivered with wit and charm, and an ending that will stay in your mind for a long, long time.

TERROR AT THE SOUND OF A WHISTLE

CAROLINE SHANNON DAVENPORT

RUNNING WILD

Terror at the Sound of a Whistle
text copyright © 2024 Reserved by Caroline Shannon Davenport
Edited by Benjamin White

Paperback ISBN: 978-1-960018-49-6
eBook ISBN: 978-1-960018-48-9

For my father and mother whose belief in my pending authorship never wavered.

HOUSES

I keep going back to doors that were never
opened—rooms that were all taped shut—places
that were seen but forbidden to enter

They were mundane doorways—but sacred spaces
Locked within were the answers to eternity—but
they allowed no admittance

They were for the dead—not the living

CHAPTER ONE

B en Beacon said, "Come on, hon, bet ya ain't never held no gun before. Come on now, just run your little paddy over that nice cool metal. Put your little finger right on that trigger. Don't that feel good, huh? Bet ya never aimed a gun at no one neither, huh?"

The terrifying man's voice I suddenly heard in my head came from a long gone time. It was a fearful jolt that bolted me back to the love of my life, James Patrick Dugan, whose parents, along with my own, were partners in crime. The four of them operated an illegal after-hours gambling casino on the first floor of our huge Victorian home.

I had convinced myself I had left all thoughts of that behind in the far-off city of my birth.

Until, that is, the day a piercing sound of a train whistle brought me to a stop at a railroad crossing in an unfamiliar industrial section of town, quickly rekindling the strong, sulfurous smell of coal dust—and filling my heart with a sharp stab of instant fear. While I watched boxcar after boxcar pass in front of me, sunlight glinting off the dashboard, forgotten

1

images—freighted out of consciousness—of Jimmy and our lives together derailed, scattering memories along the tracks of my mind.

The boxcars, with the steady click, clack, click, clack, clatter of wheels pressing rhythm down on steel, mixed with my curse of having, as near as possible, a photographic memory, resurfacing to haunt me.

It had been years, years, and years, but the realization flickered—here I was right back at another crossroad in my life, just like the one I had fled, thinking I had escaped so long ago.

Jimmy and I were reared in a household consisting of two small families with conflicted viewpoints of right and wrong. Not that they didn't know the difference, but there was always so much to consider, starting with our families' jointly chosen means of livelihood. Outcomes were often not directly anybody's fault.

There was seldom any black and white.

They said you always had to consider the whole of the situation, the vast areas of gray. Our moms did that, sometimes the dads, and often, the numerous adults that permeated our two young impressionistic lives. There were always extenuating circumstances. It was hard to separate falsehood and blame from truth and accountability. It was difficult to find something you could pin down among all the plausible excuses I grew up hearing. Only, I never believed their chosen rationale for many things—once the carnage was over.

I have no doubts that my life would have been vastly different had I not spent my upbringing in an environment where rules and blame were often arbitrary and intentions carried far too much weight. I accepted the dynamics of that complex environment as love. I had no better definition. Without my familiarity with that complexity, I wouldn't have been running headlong into adulthood trying to create the perfect lifestyle where nobody would fall off, or be pushed from, the back of a train in the dead of night.

During that skewed childhood, that train tragedy would destroy all my hopes, dreams, and plans. It caused the circle of choices to close, like the sparkly promise of toy tracks around a Christmas tree—never to expand into adult possibilities. No matter my later attempts to avoid the route, I always found myself back at the beginning—seemingly, standing in front of an empty, dark railway station with the stench of coal dust, like black death raining down, feeling the faint vibrations of boxcars with the mourning wail of a whistle echoing in the stillness of another fractured romantic relationship; once again, alone.

Wondering why.

Life certainly wouldn't have had the intrigue or the draw towards the strange and unusual that I always felt compelled to follow and found so fascinating; particularly, when it came to the men in my life—running to and from them, the good and the bad. The most enticing were always the rule-breakers, the Ten Commandment abdicators, the heavy karmic radiators, the haters and the hurters, who thought their true intentions, their heartfelt justifications, and their sincere, sorrowful regrets would somehow vindicate them from all consequences and be their saving grace.

The huge Victorian sat up on the edge of a hill, overlooking a two-lane highway. The hill was the start of an incline for a viaduct that ran over the highway. There was a long concrete stairway that led up to our porch and a door that was never used. The windows facing the road had their shades perpetually drawn closed. The house was imposing—ancient wood construction and horror-movie dark, perched on the steep rise, an abandoned aberration; a ghost house. It was the perfect foil of a false impression that suited itself to the unorthodox lives of the inhabitants.

The entrance was on the side of the house adjacent to the large parking lot, with the grunge from double train tracks that ran parallel and over that viaduct on the highway. The endless succession, from morning through night, of boxcar vibrations with soot and dust knocked loose to float with the rhythm of our daily existence—train traffic that was to prove foretelling.

Our parking lot opened at the rear, onto an angular back street, in a semi-rural area at the beginning of the outskirts of the port city of Toledo, Ohio. In the late 1940s and '50s, if you continued even farther on that main highway, out into the countryside, the flat land opened up to miles of cornfields and farmland, punctuated by a house now and then, and a few scattered small towns—the Midwestern Heartland that our imaginations saw as a much-too-distant gateway to Oz.

But Toledo was no Emerald City. It was a glass capital and industrial center that had drawn many ethnic groups from foreign lands. Situated on the shores of Lake Erie, not far from Detroit and the car industry, the English, the French, the Italians, Hungarians, Polish, and Irish came at various times to work in the factories and businesses.

People were friendly, always glad to be helpful in a neighborly way. They were hard-working and conservative. They were firm believers in the Pledge of Allegiance, Sunday school, and the courthouse. There were ladies' bridge clubs with finger sandwiches, local fairs with Betty Crocker Cook Book cakes, VFW Friday night fish fries, fire hall potluck suppers, and ballroom dancing to the big band sound.

It was a time when proper ruled. There was proper attire for any given event, proper speech, and proper action for any given situation. Ladies wore gloves, and gentlemen wore hats. Children were to be briefly seen while the depth of their silence was a measure of being raised well—conditioned not to voice an opinion.

The law that governed was, of course, always to be upheld, if only in appearance—even when it was bent—or, in our parents' case, clearly broken. Most folks didn't know about the rule-bending or, perhaps more accurately, didn't want to know. But the rule makers, the power brokers, bribe-takers, head-turners—the overlord sheepherders—they knew. It was their business to know. It was their business to profit, and business was good with every neat, white envelope full of crisp, new bank bills my father routinely delivered to the police station for the head of the city vice squad.

Graft.

Once a month, into the downtown office and up the long, imposing steps into the official, granite columned building of justice, he would go, into the bright, shining sanctuary exchanging pleasantries with the numerous staff of milling officers, detectives, and the rank and file, before finally being ushered into a private office to hand over the cash. While I often accompanied him on these visits, I usually waited outside the office, placated with a treat from the office candy bowl. As "Little Miss Inquisitive" and the ever-watchful child, albeit somewhat mystified, I, like my father, was just another lamb of sacrifice. The cash was the blood of the innocent—and not so innocent.

That small highway at the foot of our house, Woodville Road, was one of the few main arteries leading outward from the east side of the smokestack-filled city into the open and still sparsely populated landscape. Other than the highway, with its occasional array of gas stations and clusters of stores and restaurants, the roads were primarily rural. Houses were a mix of older and newer. Some were farmhouses, or once had been, with much of their farmland sold off over time for various economic reasons, but always resulting in accommodating the town's expansion into the suburbs where new houses were built

5

and bought by the more prosperous. They tended to be grouped in small handsome developments with neat and tidy lawns, patios, and flower gardens. However, none were as old or obtrusively big or utilized for the purpose ours was, or for that matter, occupied by two families who appeared to be related, but weren't.

Jimmy's family occupied an apartment on the second floor of our house while we lived on the top floor. What would have been considered a typical family environment bore no resemblance to ours whatsoever.

The covers of the ladies' magazines our mothers bought portrayed family mealtime around the dinner table, yet had nothing in common with our own. Nothing. Nor did the families we knew in our neighborhood, or those we came to know once we started school and widened our circle. They were all more closely aligned to that magazine vision of life and lifestyles. There was always the beautiful, perfectly set table, with one dad at the head, one smiling mom presiding over the perfect roast beef, or the perfectly browned and gleaming turkey, and the beaming siblings with their very large, perfect glasses of milk.

As children, we often ate together as one big family: two moms, two dads, two kids. Or, if our mothers happened to be cooking separate meals, we would strategically decide to eat with whichever mother was making what we liked best—sometimes running up and down the stairs to nibble a little at each mother's table.

If, as was the frequent case, our fathers were busy with work down in the casino, we had dinner with just our mothers. And while there might be a roast or a turkey, more likely, it was homemade noodles with beef or venison, Italian sauce, and pasta, hot dogs, and hot fudge sundaes. Maybe, just pancakes thick with Karo syrup and peanut butter. It was a time when proper ruled, but when we kids screamed our orders from within the chaotic demands for what we liked best, proper failed.

And our mothers indulged.

Our dads did not go off to work in the morning like the magazine dads, or like every other dad we came to know. They were not like dads who left with their lunch pails for the factory or their newspapers for the office.

Our dads were sleeping.

Daytime sleeping.

Unless they were still up from the night before and out in the big kitchen on Jimmy's floor with ten other people from the casino, who had stayed after the casino had closed, all crammed in around the large, yellow, Formica table laughing and talking while our moms fixed breakfast.

Either that or they were having a very late afternoon lunch and discussing someone's problem. It could be one of our relative's situations, although it took Jimmy and me a while to figure out whose relative it was, Jimmy's or mine. To us, they were all and always just aunts and uncles, but more likely, the situation or problem they were mulling over belonged to one of the renters who lived in one of the many small cabins in a compound on our property.

Our parents were more than privileged landlords to the often drifters and sometimes troubled tenants. They were the peace-keepers, advice-givers, and occasionally, caretakers. While we, their gentry children, with a natural knack for opportunistic eavesdropping, were privy to all their private lives.

Born one month apart, with a natural affinity for each other since toddlerhood, Jimmy and I cleaved together to form an unbreakable bond. In the place and period we were raised, we were an anomaly. Once in school, we quickly realized it, no

7

longer set apart from other children who had parents who lived respectable middle-class lives, went to church, and organized ice cream socials.

I knew we were different, but I always wanted to believe we weren't.

I always wanted to believe in magic, like the rabbit I loved and nurtured with Jimmy, that we materialized out of a black hat. I wanted magic instead of what I came to discover in the hard, cold reality—the sacrificed blood of the innocent. I wanted the mystical, magical tricks, but instead I learned the lessons on the back of someone's sleight of hand.

And I knew that life was not as it seemed. I knew it could be shattered in an instant, but I always wanted it to be as beautiful as the moments we spent once upon a fairytale time. We were our mothers' precious darlings, our fathers' innocent charges, and each other's twinned windows into the world. There were moments that were golden; they were gossamer, full of satin ribbon ties that wrapped us up in warmth, like the hollow of sweetness in a lover's embrace and held us securely in laughter and joy—but those moments were fleeting.

There were reality shocks, chaos, and fear that interrupted our charmed childhood. We realized that the adult world's platitudes and conventions were often fakeries—that honesty was in short supply, that appearances were deceiving, and trust was arbitrary.

That proper was a facade.

Of the two of us, Jimmy understood more clearly early on. I was the one who wanted to believe in the stardust—the falling streams of light in the wondrous bursts of illegal fireworks our fathers displayed every Fourth of July—long after the sparkle fell to earth and died.

And suddenly the thoughts, hopes, and perceptions once forced to vacate when reality moved in were unpacking themselves from old memories, out of sentimental suitcases, and from the captivity of emotional cardboard boxes. The sounds and smells had awakened long-forgotten scenes tucked someplace deep inside the recesses of my subconscious. As I went about my routine all day, thoughts of my childhood floated in and out. Memories came full-blown, dropping me back in time, obscuring the present, and pushing me into the past.

So that evening, after my encounter at the railroad crossing, as I sat at my desk, husband off on another relentless business trip, in my lovely, cavernous castle of a home, in my most lonely state, just me and only me, I heard it in my head once again.

Very distinctly.

The shrill train whistle.

Now, hours later, it seemed like several lifetimes had elapsed. I sipped a glass of wine while I sat in front of my computer screen, staring off into space, and I heard the voice again.

My childish voice.

My little girl voice.

It was clear and direct and very insistent on being heard. She had a wedding on her mind. She wanted to go back to where it started. The bonding, knowing what it was like to have someone always by your side, someone who was always there to take your side—someone who knew the depth and breadth of you, who understood your heart, and your mind, and your soul.

I heard her say, "It was the year we were almost five."

Jimmy had told her, "Hey, I got this idea, know what we could do?"

As she remembered, I listened.

And she told me about how it was way back then; about those flawed people I loved so dearly; about Jimmy, about me,

9

about Jimmy and me; about everything I had walled up, flooded over in the dark valley of my being, and placed far away on the far side of the protective moat I had built around myself.

She told me the truth of what had happened, so long ago, in that elicit house on the edge of a hill.

And as I listened, I typed.

CHAPTER TWO

"Hey, I got this idea. Know what we could do?"

"Nuh-unh," I said.

"'Member that show we saw 'bout those Injuns makin' that pact an' bein' blood brothers an' all?"

"Yeah."

"'Member how the pact was so they'd never trust nobody better than each other, an' they'd be real stronger, an' nobody'd hardly ever hurt 'em cause they'd be sworn to protect each other?"

"Yeah."

"We could do that," Jimmy said. "Only 'stead of blood brothers, we could make it like we was wedded forever!"

"Yeah! Till we'd get bigger an' wedded for real." I said.

"Only it'd be 'ficial between us now," Jimmy said. "And we could never tell each other no lies or nothin'. Ya know what else?" Jimmy said.

"Nuh-uh," I said.

"It'd be like in the movies, too, that if ya broke it, your spirit would be alone forever. Just roamin' 'round alone forever!"

11

"Yeah, but we'd never break it!"

So, Jimmy got a razor blade from his dad's medicine chest, and we went out in this field that was our favorite place. It was this field where some company dumped all this dirt once. They just left it. It was hilly, and grew all this grass and flowers, and had these big trees, and a bunch of small ones that looked like palm trees. My mom said they were Sumac. They looked like these pictures Jimmy and me saw one time in a book about this island in the ocean. Jimmy and me said, when we got big, we would go to the real islands as honeymooners. So that's why we wanted to do it in this field. It would look just like real.

We made this sort of altar, like they have in churches. I brought the Bible my grandmother got for me when I was born. We couldn't read it, or nothing yet, but some stuff we knew by heart.

We picked these flowers that were daisies and put them all over the place. I made a round thing of them to put in my hair like the women in the pictures did, those native ladies on that island. I wore this dress that Jimmy liked that was white with these baby, tiny flowers on it. It was like a real wedding dress. We had to be careful, so we didn't get blood on it.

Jimmy took some whiskey his dad had in his cabinet that was full of lots of different kinds of this liquor. It would be like in the movies with the Indians that drank this stuff. My mom said it was probably so them Indians would get in a trance and not feel any pain. It was supposed to make you in your spirit. In the movie, their souls were meeting. So that's what Jimmy and me were going to do. We were going to make our souls be wedded.

We got our moms to pack us this picnic lunch to take. Lots of times, they would do it. They would put sandwiches, and apples, and cookies, and stuff in a basket for us. We asked them to make it special, 'cause we were having a special celebration party. We didn't tell them what though. We said it was secret. They just laughed.

Jimmy said, "Aw, they just probably think it's just some nutty kid stuff!"

When they got done fixing it, we went out to the field. First, Jimmy said we should drink some of the whiskey. I thought it tasted really awful. It made my breath almost go away.

"Ya gotta glub it fast," Jimmy said.

I tried, but I started coughing.

"Not that fast, dummy! Watch me." Then Jimmy started coughing.

"Yuck! How come grownups like this dumb stuff?" I said.

"Cause it's 'poseta make ya feel good."

While we were picking all those daisy flowers, I started feeling dizzy. Jimmy said he felt like that too. So we drank some more, but not a lot. Jimmy said it would make you sick if you drank too much—like once when we sneaked down and saw some grownups get after the casino. Some guy threw up in our parking lot.

There were big clouds in the sky. They were floating along real nice. So we started watching them under this tree. We were lying on our backs, staring straight up at them. I started feeling like we could almost be a cloud.

"It feels like we're up there in 'em," Jimmy said.

"Yeah, sort of like we're movin', comin' right up next to 'em like there's no space between us. S'pose God's up there watchin' us?" I said.

"Maybe. He's 'poseta know everything."

"Yeah. Only we're 'poseta be sittin' up makin' chant sounds like in the movie," I said. "That's what's 'poseta really put ya in your spirit an' get God to be here. Only, how we gonna know if we're in the spirit?" I said.

"You're jus' 'poseta know dummy!" Jimmy said.

Jimmy said we should drink more of that whiskey and make pledges like the Indians did. The Indians sat so they would be facing each other. They held up their hands like Indians do when they say "how" like they're greeting each other. They made the pledges to be blood brothers forever. Jimmy said we should put our hands over our hearts as you do for the flag—just to make double-sure we would never break it.

"You hafta swear to never break the pledge or lie," Jimmy said. "I always swear to never break the pledge or lie," Jimmy said first. "Now, you."

"I always swear to never break the pledge an' not lie," I said. "Now we hafta say how this'll mean we'll be wedded forever. I promise—" I started.

"Wait! You hafta say your name," Jimmy said.

"Okay, I, Caroline."

"No! Your real name, dummy. The whole thing, like at weddings."

"Okay, Caroline, I mean, Caroline Shannon Davenport, I promise to be wedded to Jimmy—"

"James!"

"I mean, to James Patrick Dugan, all my life forever."

"Until you die, say."

"Until I die. Now you."

"I, James Patrick Dugan, promise to be wedded to Caroline Shannon Davenport, all my life forever."

"Now, do we do the trance to make it sealed?" I asked.

"Yeah, but first, we hafta kiss, then start."

"Now, who's gonna start?" I asked after the kiss.

"I'll start," Jimmy said. "Let's say, I go I go I ga I ga."

"Yeah! I ga I ga u."

"Yeah, then I ga I ga u ga. An' just keep saying it." Jimmy said.

At first, it seemed kind of dumb. Then, we started swaying

back and forth with the sound, both sayin' it together, and it started feeling real nice. "I ga I ga u ga we ga. I ga I ga u ga we ga. I ga u ga we ga u ga we ga. I ga I ga u ga we ga."

The sound started seeming like it was all around us after a while. "I ga I ga u ga we ga. I ga I ga u ga we ga. I ga I ga u ga we ga."

Jimmy and I were holding hands. It was just going on, and on, and on. I ga I ga u ga we ga.

Jimmy took this razor blade, and cut his arm, just like making a nick. I took it and cut mine, tiny. We held our arms together tight and kept doing it. "I ga I ga u ga we ga."

It hardly hurt at all! It was like we were not even there, but someplace else. It was like we were watching it happen, but not feeling nothing.

Finally, we just stopped because it seemed like it was done. We had planned to do this other stuff—these prayers and all.

"Anyways, Injuns don't say bible prayers," Jimmy said.

"Yeah, only I like that one 'bout God bein' merciful an' blessin' an' causin' his face to shine on you. Mom said you don't have to say the words anyhow. All that you have to do is be thinkin' it. Like we were doin'. Maybe that's how come it felt like that, cause God was there listening even though we wasn't saying it in bible talk?" I said.

"Yeah," Jimmy said. "That's how come it'll be forever."

So we got kid married.

Jimmy said it didn't matter that we were just kids. Jimmy said it would still be forever. I never said anything, but I kept wondering about that like I wanted not to be scared. Only, what if something happened, like with my real dad, that would make it not forever?

Well, my dad now was my real dad and everything. I mean, he acted like a dad, not like the other one that my mom didn't talk about, but who I remembered. He was there from when I was first born and a baby. He held me tight and would laugh into my face, seeing into me close up, so I felt into his blue eyes like warm sea water all around. He smelled good and could hum in my ear and felt strong. I thought.

He was silly, too. He could play like he was a kid. It was fun. We would play chase and catch. But he was fast, and I got caught. Mostly. Once, I got him. Not really. I knew he made it so I could do the catching. He said I was beautiful and could catch anything I wanted.

He cried once. He hit Mom once, too. I think Jimmy's dad, Big Jim, and my now dad, made him go away. It was before my mom got a divorce from him she told me. It was when I was real little. He came to work for Big Jim and my now dad, as the runner of the bar. He was a bartender like his dad, my grandfather, who I only kind of remembered. Mom said my grandfather was Irish like Big Jim and owned a tavern. Only, it was a *legal* place, not like with Big Jim and my now dad.

Nobody thought we knew, but Jimmy and me heard them talking when we were listening behind the door one night about how the casino should be legal. That's how we found out about my before dad being a drinker. Only, my mom didn't know until after she was married to him, on account of him being sick like my mom was when they were in the tubercular hospital, and him not drinking until later. That was before my now dad became my real dad. I never wanted him to go away. Nobody could lose two dads. So I guessed Jimmy was right. Nothing would go wrong.

We would be wedded forever.

CHAPTER THREE

The most important thing was you had to stick with the other one, no matter what. After the marriage thing we did, this dumb, old kindergarten teacher tried to make us not stick together, but make us sit way apart from each other. Well, she wasn't really old-old, but older than our moms.

Our moms had hair that was styled. My mom's was dark red and curled. Jimmy's mom had dark brown and short hair. It was parted on the side, real nice and neat looking. They always wore lipstick, and had pretty skin, and were so soft like you could just sink right into them. They smelled real good, like powder and perfume.

My dad said that Jimmy's mom, Pauline, was less frilly than my mom, Margie. He said she was more conservative. Pauline wore penny loafers with her nylons, and skirts, and cardigans, or white blouses. She never wore make-up, just lipstick. She was beautiful with brown eyes. Like love eyes. She was the one that smelled like baby powder when she would lean over you to look at something with you or serve you breakfast. My mom was lacy and silky and smelled like roses. My dad said she was like a movie star with her smile like a bubble. She laughed a lot and would kiss you for no reason.

This teacher looked like she would never kiss anybody when she was being regular, and not being sugary trying to get you to like her. She was wrinkly, and had her hair short and curly messy, with no lipstick even. Our moms were thin, but she was kind of wide like a desk, with worn-down heels on her shoes, like at a slant, from walking.

Boy, we didn't like her right from the start when she started saying all this phony-baloney stuff about how cute we were and going on about how we looked like little twins, and how sweet, and patting us on the head. Well, maybe I kind of liked her at the very, very first when she was smiling a lot. I thought something was wrong with her hip was why she walked funny, and maybe it hurt and made her seem mean when she wasn't trying to be nice on purpose.

Jimmy said no. She was just mean. He didn't care why. She was putting this big show on for our moms because they didn't really want to leave us. Then after they left, she started getting bossy and telling Jimmy and me that we had to play with all these other kids instead of only each other. She was making her voice sound sugary, too. Jimmy said it was to get us to do what she wanted.

"Jimmy dear, why don't you go over with the other boys and play? They're over there building something with all those nice blocks. Caroline, you come with me," she said.

She took my hand and started having me meet all these other girls. A couple of them were pretty nice. One girl was Janet. She was shy. She was nice, too. Only, some of them were bossy. This one named Cheryl that had on this red ruffle dress with dots all over it was real, real bossy. She started telling everybody that we were going to play this doll game, and who could be the mother and father, and who would get to be the bigger sisters, and who would get to be the little sisters, and who would have to be the little brothers. Janet and I had to be the brothers. I didn't care anyhow, though. I didn't want to play their stupid game.

Janet and I found a puzzle in a box of toys and started putting it together. I kept watching Jimmy. He was sitting there watching these boys try to build a building. Most of them were trying to be show-offs, being smarty over who could get the next block on faster, saying how they all knew how to do it better. Every time it would fall over or something, they would start yelling at each other like a bunch of sissy babies.

Boy, Jimmy hated it.

Then the teacher said she would read this story and told us to sit in the circle on the floor around her in these little chairs. Jimmy said they were baby chairs. I liked them. They were cute. Jimmy said we didn't need baby chairs. We were bigger and smarter.

Anyway, when Jimmy and me started to pull our chairs up, right in front of all these kids, the teacher told us we couldn't sit together. "Jimmy and Caroline, you two sit next to someone new."

Jimmy was mad.

Later, when we had to take naps like real babies on these little rugs, she wouldn't let Jimmy and me be together.

When our moms came to get us, she told them how we didn't want to play with the other kids. And this stuff about how we were too shy and needed to be with other kids more. She said it right in front of everybody, practically like we were dummies or something. Jimmy and me never wanted to go back. Only, we didn't want to be sissies, neither. The next day it was worse. We couldn't look at each other. She kept watching us like she was waiting for one of us to try to get next to the other one.

When we had recess time, Jimmy and me and Janet and this other boy, Jerry, who Jimmy kind of liked, went to play on the swings together. We were swinging, and these two boys came over. They started calling Jimmy and Jerry sissies for playing with us girls. One of them that was bigger pushed Jerry. Jerry pushed him back, too, even though he was smaller. Only, the kid pushed him harder and knocked him down. Jimmy got in front of Jerry then—and told the kid he better leave us alone.

"Yeah, ya gonna make me?" the kid said, looking mean.

"Yeah," Jimmy said, looking mean right back.

This kid started laughing because he didn't think Jimmy would do anything. He started to walk away. Jimmy grabbed him by the arm and punched him good. Then, they were really fighting in the gravel by the swings.

The playground teacher came running over and pulled them apart. "You boys stop this instant!"

She grabbed Jimmy and that kid by the arms. The kid started screaming about how Jimmy hit him first. "He started it!"

Jimmy wouldn't say anything. The other kid's face was bloodied up. So the teacher started shaking Jimmy.

"Why'd you hit him?" she said, looking mean.

Jimmy wouldn't say anything. I knew he was trying not to bawl. The other kid was bawling all over the place. I couldn't stand it because it wasn't fair.

"It wasn't Jimmy's fault!" I said.

"Just be quiet, Caroline. Everybody back inside. All right, stop crying, Mark. Jimmy, you brush your clothes off. Go back in with the rest while I take Mark to the nurse's station. I'll talk to you later!" she said.

This other teacher came. She stayed with us in our room for a while, until ours got back with Mark. The nurse put a bandage on him, but his face was already swollen up looking.

His mom came to get him. He started putting on this big act. We could hear them outside the door to our room. Boy, was he a liar. He was acting like it was all Jimmy's fault. His mother got mad. She was saying at the teacher how her kid could have been blinded or something, and why wasn't the teacher watching better.

When the mother left, the teacher came back in. She said she wanted to see Jimmy out in the hall.

"The rest of you kids just be good, and I'll read a story in a minute."

She took Jimmy outside. She closed the classroom door, but we could still hear them.

"All right, Jimmy, why did you hit Mark?" she asked.

"Cause he called Jerry an' me sissies."

"Oh, so that's any reason to nearly blind someone? Jimmy, did you see what you did to Mark's face? His mother's taking him to the doctor. Jimmy, are you listening to me? Look at me! Do you hear me? Answer me!"

"Yeah!"

"Don't act smart with me, young man. You go back in the room. When your mother gets here, I'm going to have a talk with her!"

So when Big Jim and my dad and our moms came to get us, just our moms came inside. Jimmy and me had to go out to sit in the car with our dads until they got done talking to the teacher. Our dads didn't say anything to us. But I knew we were in trouble. When our moms came out of the school and got in the car, I couldn't stand it anymore, and started crying.

"I don't care; I don't ever wanna go back to that dumb sc-school no more!" I said.

"All right, let's hear it, what happened?" Pauline, Jimmy's mom said.

"It was-was-n't Jimmy's fa-ult. That dumb k-k-id started it!"

I said.

"Okay, okay, calm down," Mom said, "don't cry."

"Jimmy, why'd you hit that kid? Lord, Jim, his mother's ready to sue the school!" Pauline said, her eyes going all bulgy.

"He started it!" Jimmy said. "Caroline an' this kid, Jerry, an' this other girl, Janet, an' me were playin' on the swings, an' he comes over and starts callin' Jerry an' me sissies cause we were playin' with girls. And he pushed Jerry down!"

"Yeah, right in the gravel! Jerry was smaller than him, too! By a whole lot!" I said.

"So I punched him," Jimmy said.

Pauline said. "Jimmy, you can't go around hitting people even if you are right! Did you tell the teacher what happened? She seemed to think everything was your fault."

"Yeah, but she wouldn't listen. She started blamin' Jimmy right away!" I said.

"I don't wanna go back there, either!" Jimmy said.

"Me neither!" I said.

"Now look, you kids have to go to school," my mom said.

"Unh-unh," I said. "Kindergarten's just extra! You said so."

"Oh, brother! You two never forget a thing, do you? Look, we'll talk about this later," my mom said. "Let's just go home and get cleaned up, and everyone calm down. After supper, we'll discuss it."

Jimmy's dad, Big Jim, started the car. It got real quiet. At supper, our moms and dads didn't say anything more about it.

"Bet they're gonna discuss it now," Jimmy said, after we got done eating when we went into Jimmy's room to play. So, we sneaked back into the living room outside the kitchen to listen.

"Frankly, I don't think that teacher likes the kids!" Pauline said.

Jimmy's dad started kind of laughing but trying not to. "Sounds like the kid deserved it to me," he said.

"Maybe we should go have another talk with her?" my mom said.

"What's that going to do? You think the kids are going to like her any better?" Big Jim asked.

"But Jim, the kids have to go to school. They're going to have to learn to get along with other kids!" Pauline said.

"I'm not disagreeing with you. But the fact remains that the kids aren't too crazy about the teacher, and the teacher isn't too crazy about the kids. Now, if you try pushing this situation, you're liable to end up with them hating school before they even get into first grade!"

"I agree," my dad said. "I think we should leave the kids at home. They've only got one more year anyway before they have to go. Why rush their freedom?"

"Well, I'm still worried about this shyness business," Pauline said.

"So am I," Mom said. "You guys didn't see those kids when we first took them in that room. Caroline had herself nearly glued to Jimmy's side when we left. God, they looked like they were nearly terrified!"

"Did you ask them about it?" my dad said.

"Sure, but a lot of good it did! They denied it like crazy. Jimmy stood right there and said, 'wasn't either scared.' And Caroline parrots him," Mom said.

"Well, for God's sake, what do you expect? They've been raised together. They've never been around other children their own age," my dad said.

"Look, I don't think there is any reason for us to get riled over this," Big Jim said. "So next year they'll get a different teacher. They're not going to be five until a few more months as it is. They'll be a little older then. If there's a problem, we'll take care of it later. Let 'em stay home!"

He got up and took his coffee with this little glass of brandy he had after supper, then went into the study room with my dad, while Mom and Pauline did the dishes.

Boy, were we glad! I said I never wanted to go to school again. Jimmy said we would have to anyway next year. "But we don't have to like it none. They can't make us like those phony ol' kids. Boy, what a bunch of babies." Jimmy said.

"Janet was nice, though. So was that Jerry kid." I said.

"Yeah, but ya couldn't trust 'em, I bet," Jimmy said.

"I betcha could Janet!" I said.

"Oh yeah? Then how come she never said nothin' when that dumb Mark was sayin' I started it?"

"Well, she was just scared is all. That Jerry was being brave!"

"Oh yeah! He never said nothin' neither!" Jimmy said.

"You didn't think I wasn't gonna say nothin' didja?" I asked. "Didja?"

"Course not, dummy!"

"Was I brave?" I said.

"Yeah, pretty brave. But boy, were you ever scared!"

"Was not!"

"Yeah you were."

"You were scared, too!"

"Was not!" Jimmy said.

I said maybe our moms would teach us at home. Jimmy said not to be dumb, that the police would make you go. It was a law. Only, what our dads' friend, Bo Bo, said once, was that what our dads did was against the law, and the police didn't make our dads do nothing!

Jimmy said he guessed that was different. The police got paid money by our dads to let them do it. They probably didn't do it for kids. We had to get grown up first. So we were just going to have to go to school and be brave.

I didn't like having to be brave.

24

CHAPTER FOUR

O ur house was high up on a hill with no yard. It only had a front porch with a door that had tall windows on each side that you couldn't see through from outside because they had white shades that were always pulled down. There were concrete steps going down to the sidewalk by the highway below. On the side of our house, right after our big gravel drive-way, were train tracks that crossed the highway, but, so the trains wouldn't stop traffic, my mom said, they built a bridge, a viaduct. So that was why we were on a hill. The men who built the highway had to cut out the land in front of our house like a tunnel under the viaduct for the trains to go over the top. The highway, like our house, was old from horse and buggy days my mom said.

Jimmy and I liked to play pretend games about more than anything. Our favorite was to pretend we could make a dream that was real. It'd be a special place where bad things would never happen, where nobody would get hurt or die. Behind our house, way out in the back, there was a dinky road with some houses on it that had a bunch of land around them like ours. So that is where we played. Those fields, and hills, and the creek by our house made it pretty easy to think up imaginary stuff.

This creek wasn't too good, though. It was pretty disgusting, really. We lived kind of out in the country. My dad said it was the outskirts. There was this oil refinery nearby, but not too close. It had big smokestacks, where sometimes white clouds of rotten egg smelly stuff came out, and they would dump all this stinky vomit oil gunk in the creek that would stay in the water. Sometimes the water was clear when they weren't dumping. But most times, it was pretty bad.

When they were dumping, it was pretty hard to pretend the creek was the Nile, or anyplace special like our moms told us about, with it smelling like gasoline awful. The water would get oily slimy. It would have these colors in it that my mom called fluorescent.

One time we found a dead otter and told our moms. They and our dads came to look. It made me cry when we were telling it and again when we were looking at it. I was really sad —Jimmy too. The poor otter. His fur was matted in this awful slime oil and he was laying up on the edge of the water. My mom said the oil must of suffocated him, and he crawled up and died. Our parents were mad. My dad got all red in the face. He said bad words about the oil company and said he was going to talk to people about the company killing wildlife. Dad told us not to touch the otter and that the people, the bastards, didn't give a shit—it was just a cheap place to dump.

When it was real nasty hot or cold, snowing, or blowing real bad outside, we would play inside the house. Although in the summer, if it was just raining with no lightning or thunder, we would get to play outside in it. We would put on our swimsuits when the rain was coming down nice, run into it, and jump puddles. We would play this game of who could stand the longest under the eave of the house where the drain pipe was missing. The water would be coming down real hard and it would almost knock you over like it was Niagara Falls. Jimmy would play like he was going over in a barrel, or like he was Houdini.

He was always doing magic tricks so he could be famous someday.

He was going to be a famous magician.

Inside our house had three floors with a lot of rooms. My dad said the guy that built it must not have been able to decide when to quit building. We sometimes would play on the stairs pretending they were mountains we had to climb, making up adventures. It was a long flight of stairs, and they went up from the first floor to the third story. The first floor was where the casino was and we weren't allowed to play there. There was a door into the casino at the foot of the stairs, but we weren't allowed to open it, though.

On the first floor we got to go into the casino sometimes but only played in the family rooms on the other two floors. Those rooms on our family's floors formed a circle around the stairway coming up into the middle of the house.

Mom said the front entrance got changed to be on the side of the house, and that made the main staircase the one we used. But there were some other stairs that nobody knew about. They came up and had a door on the second floor where Jimmy's family lived. That door opened in a big hallway next to Jimmy's room. Pauline used the stairway to store Christmas decoration stuff. The door was kept locked.

But that wasn't the only door that was always locked. Our dads kept that front door always bolted. And where the casino was, my mom made these black drapes of silky stuff to hang.

They covered the entrance that people used to use so you couldn't see it. It just looked like a wall of pretty curtains inside. We only used that door once. When we had to get out the front way in a hurry, when we were gonna be killed.

CHAPTER FIVE

On Jimmy's mom and dad's floor, the second floor, you could go into their kitchen where everything happened that we weren't supposed to know. At the top of the stairs, you turned, and then walked down this hall. At the end of the hall, there was a little window where you had to turn to go straight into the kitchen. Across from the window was a door that led up more stairs onto my mom and dad's and my floor. Except, most people didn't go up to our floor. Jimmy's kitchen was where everybody went.

Sometimes, before people went in, they liked to stop and look out the little window. There was a big tree right outside it, and you could see down into the backyard where there was pretty grass with flowers and all the renters' cabins. Everybody called it the courtyard. It had lawn chairs and tables.

In the kitchen, there was another window, but it just looked down into the parking lot and out to the train tracks that ran past our house on the side, the viaduct, and the dinky back road. The parents liked it, especially our dads. They could see who was coming and going. In case it was bad guys.

After the kitchen, was Jimmy's living room with another bigger window. Our house had lots of windows so you could see everywhere. Jimmy's mom and dad's bedroom and study was in the front of the house after the living room, and the windows looked down on that big highway below. My bedroom and my mom and dad's bedroom, on the very top floor, did too.

Jimmy and me used to watch out of them if it rained a bunch at once, coming fast. The viaduct that the trains ran over would flood underneath on account of the highway going down so low. Dad said they cut it too deep, and it didn't have good drainage.

We'd run upstairs in a hurry if it was raining and starting to downpour, so we could see what people would do. We made bets. Some would back up and turn around, some would creep up like they were going to try to get through, and then back up, but some dumb people would drive real fast and get stuck. Jimmy said they were idiots like his dad said. His dad said there was always somebody trying to beat the odds, willing to gamble. The people in the car would have to wade out. Mom said their cars would be ruined. I thought it was sad.

Jimmy's room was on the other side of the house, off that hallway I told you about, where that door was, to the stairs nobody used that went down to the front of the house. Pauline said a long time ago, the stairs were to come up from what was somebody's living room. Now, it was full of lots of tables and chairs in the casino. I wished it could be our big living room, like I saw in this book, with all these beautiful couches and pillars like for kings and queens to live in.

Jimmy's room had big windows close together in one place. Jimmy had a desk there where we would draw and paint pictures and make stuff. The windows made it like being in a treehouse, so we could look outside at the highway and the neighbor's big house next door before they tore it down. Then, on the other side of Jimmy's room was a bathroom. The bathroom had two doors. One that was for Jimmy's room and one that you could open into that hallway, next to that little window everybody looked out. The bathroom was right across from the kitchen. That is what I meant when I said the rooms on each floor went around in kind of a circle. My floor was the top, like Jimmy's, only different, and my mom's kitchen wasn't as big.

We weren't allowed into the first-floor casino place much. Just sometimes in the daytime, if they were cleaning and delivering stuff like meat, and liquor, or something, and if our dads were down there. It was closed till late night. It was what people called the casino, but our dad's called the club, where they played cards and had food and drinks. They danced too. Somebody was killed there before our dads got it. Later, somebody died in it again.

The casino was the only place we weren't allowed to go in the house. Outside, we couldn't go over to where we would have to cross the railroad tracks. There were two sets of train tracks after our big parking lot you could park about a hundred cars in. No kidding! If you didn't know, you would probably think it was for the renters who lived in the cabins that our dads owned so that they could park their cars there. Only, that was just part of why. It was really on account of the club that nobody was supposed to know about, but they did. My dad said the churches didn't like it, so everybody had to be quiet about it, and it was why it couldn't be legal.

Jimmy and I weren't blood-related, really. It was just like we were. Everybody was always saying we looked just like each other. We had the same color hair and eyes. Mom said we were both pixie looking, so that was why. Jimmy was older by a month, almost. His birthday was in November and mine was in December. My mom said they were important birthdays. My

31

mom said we were born almost at the holiest time of the year. She said that could mean we might even get famous one day. We made a pact that if we did, whoever got famous first, would make the other one famous next.

We never saw our dads much. They were busy with running everything for everybody our moms said. I mean, we liked them all right and all, but they just never said much. They were pretty quiet and big. Especially Jimmy's dad. He was tall and had gray hair, and was handsome, and wore dark glasses all the time. So you never knew what he was looking at or thinking. Pauline said bright light hurt his eyes was why. People would always act respectful around him. When he would come into a room, it would get real quiet.

My dad was Merlin, but everybody called him Merle; he was kind of like Big Jim, but in another way. He was bigger around and had blond wavy hair, and big smiles, and white beautiful teeth. He made a lot of jokes and had blue eyes that my mom said twinkled, but when he would start getting serious, people would get quiet, too, just like for Jimmy's dad.

Our dads always acted sort of different around us, like they didn't know what to say. Jimmy said it was that they probably didn't know many kids—that was what Pauline said, anyway. My mom showed me pictures once of my dad when he was little. Jimmy had a picture of his dad, but we couldn't imagine them ever being kids. It seemed dumb.

We were mostly with our moms. They were the ones that told us what we were supposed to do. We didn't have lots of rules. They thought we were pretty terrific, so we got to do lots of stuff. We had favorite things we really liked that they would fix to eat. Pauline made terrific French toast with cinnamon. We would put butter, and lots of gooey ol' peanut butter on it, then Karo syrup on top. It was our favorite. Sometimes my mom would make hot fudge sundaes with double hot fudge, lots of whipped cream, and a cherry—but no nuts. We hated nuts. They would just get stuck in your teeth.

Then sometimes for supper, Pauline made this spaghetti sauce that would cook all day long. They were always cooking or making something. My dad said the house always smelled like it was Sunday dinner from Pauline's kitchen and a bakery on our floor. I liked the smell of Pauline's homemade chicken soup. And Jimmy liked the smell of butterscotch from my mom's pies best.

We got to grow things in the summer, in a garden way out back. It was behind our house and the cabins. Jimmy's dad helped us plant it. He was good at making things grow. Jimmy's dad would go outside when it was just starting to get warm and show us how to get dandelions out of the ground. We got to have dandelion salads. Pauline made these green tomatoes fried in olive oil that Jimmy's dad liked. Mom made sandwiches with a lot of butter and brown sugar sprinkled with water.

Our moms were lots of fun. They would hardly ever get mad at us. Mostly, they would just act like they were. We would catch them trying not to laugh like it was killing them to hold it in. They would be scolding us for something, but we would see them starting to grin. They would be yelling at us— but we would know they wanted to get out of the room fast. We would hear them giggling after they left. *Was it ever funny!*

The only times they would get mad would be when we were *fraying nerves* or *trying patience*. Still, they would never get real mad. Some grownups never get real mad, like looking at you squinty and hate-like, like they could just kill you, or they're going to hate you for about a billion years. When we got in a lot of trouble, though, was when they would say they were going to talk to our dads. Only, they never did. Our dads had more important stuff to do. They had to take care of every-body's problems, and that club downstairs, and make sure they were ready in case there was a big bust, or else everybody could get in bad trouble. Our mom's jobs were supposed to be taking care of us. Our moms said we were pretty good, though, except sometimes my mom said we could get carried too much away.

One time was when Jimmy and I got in this fight in a rental cabin after some people moved out. The door was open, so we just went in to look. The people had left this coffee, flour, and stuff in big cans on the counter.

Jimmy started it.

He always started it.

Mostly.

But this time, he started it. He grabbed a whole handful of flour and hit me good in the head.

WHOP.

"We're gonna get it!" I said.

He just stood there giggling at me, so I got him back, good. *WHOP.*

Then he got me. *WHOP. WHOP.*

So I got him again. *WHOP. WHOP. WHOP.*

Then he got me. *WHOP. WHOP. WHOP. WHOP. WHOP.*

Then, we really got each other a whole lot of times.

Boy, were we white! It was all in our hair and shoes. It was all over the place. It got all over a big ol' stuffed velvety black chair, and on this rug, and on the floor. Jimmy and I were just starting to try to clean it up when our moms found us.

Boy, were they mad! They made us take baths and stay inside, and we couldn't be together, either. They made me stay upstairs and Jimmy down in his room. We were supposed to be thinking about what a mess we made while they were in the cabin, cleaning it up. We felt really bad. I thought they would be mad for a really long time.

Only later, we heard them telling somebody about it,

laughing real good. They would do that a lot. When it was happening, it wasn't funny. Later, when they would be telling about it, it would get funny.

They both could tell a story to make people laugh, and when they told it together, well—it just, just seemed twice as funny. There was one story they would tell a whole bunch about the rabbits and Uncle Tommy.

Uncle Tommy was really Jimmy's uncle, but he was mine, too. Uncle Tommy was one of our favorite people, and he was always sending us these terrific presents, and clear from New York. That was where he lived. My dad said he was a big shot attorney there, and he was always having his picture in the paper, nationally. Mom said they were real expensive presents.

Jimmy and I were always imagining what New York must be like. We figured it was full of big stores that were extra tall, and sparkle looking, and had bunches of toys. It was like nothing you could ever guess that would just go on and on and on forever and ever—stores and toys that would go on forever until you couldn't even see them no more.

Even on Valentine's Day, we would get something special. Jimmy would get something like a truck, or something made special, filled with all this terrific chewy candy he liked best. It would be wrapped in this red, bright, crinkle paper that would make you go dizzy. I would get these chocolate creams my mom said were made by hand in Europe. If you bit one and looked, the creamy stuff would be oozy, and the chocolate would get melty like a dream taste. They would be in big, big, heart-shaped boxes with lace and downy feeling red stuff.

One year, on one of the boxes, was this doll with a real china head. Mom said the dress was made out of red shiny silk stuff like ribbon. That is the year Mom said we were going to be spoiled forever for life if presents weren't always the best.

Boy, you should have seen what we would get for a big

holiday like Christmas. Jimmy and I would start going nuts when it started getting close, waiting for the mailman. Uncle Tommy would send giant dolls and panda bears and trucks. And toys that would make noises, and animals that would dance, and play songs. They would be wrapped with big bows, and in lots of this really, really, bright paper.

But by far the best gifts were the live things he sent. That is where the rabbit story came from. One year when we were still five, he sent a whole twelve baby bunnies for Easter. It was when we were having a pretty terrible snowstorm, and the mailman called and told Pauline that he wasn't going to deliver them because he said, "they were awful real sick, madam."

That was what Pauline told Jimmy's dad when she was explaining why he had to go get them in the storm. He was putting on heavy boots and clothes, and he was saying bad words about Uncle Tommy that we weren't supposed to hear.

My mom and Pauline made a pen for the rabbits, in a part of that big hallway that was by Jimmy's room. It was real wide and had a door on one side, so you might have just thought it was a closet. It was good because there weren't any drafts that could get in. They took this little wooden diamond spring fence that could be pulled out to be wider so the bunnies would stay in one spot. They put it across part of the hall, and put blankets and papers down, and then brought up a hot wire electric heater to keep them warm. Pauline said it was just like an incubator.

The bunnies were sick, and they kept going to the bathroom all over, real runny. Mom and Pauline called a doctor for animals. He said to give them peppermint just like they gave us when Jimmy and I would get stomach aches. They had to give it to the bunnies in an eyedropper all night, and also this baby food drink.

Jimmy and I had to go to bed, but we couldn't sleep. So

finally, we got to stay with our pillows and blankets just outside the hall until morning next to the door and the bunnies. Mom and Pauline kept coming in the middle of the night to tell us how the bunnies were because we still couldn't sleep. In the morning, we didn't have a whole twelve left anymore, but we still had plenty, Mom said.

Our dads, and Duffy, this handyman, made a big pen outside for them when it got warmer. It was big enough, although, after the bunnies got bigger, our moms said we had to choose one, because the rest had to go live on a farm of some people our dads knew. The parents said the bunnies would be happier there. Besides, they were getting too hard to take care of anymore. We thought they were pretty neat! Our moms really liked them, too, and our dads really did, too, except we heard them talking about how they would like to strangle Uncle Tommy for sending them. Not really, though.

By having to choose one bunny is how Jimmy got Thoth. Jimmy wanted to keep Thoth because he was the biggest. He got the name Thoth on account of it meaning the inventor of magic and being an Egyptian God. This friend of ours, Penny, who was a renter, was the one that thought up the name. She was young and real smart. And sort of married to a woman who was like a guy. On account of them living in the same cabin, it got pretty bad later with them, like our dad's friend warned our dads it would. He called 'em a bad word. But I didn't care. I loved her.

Anyway, she said we could have named him Hermes because it meant the same God, only in Greek. We liked Thoth better. It was the best name because Jimmy wanted Thoth to be his special rabbit to use in his magic trick act.

How the magic act started was when Uncle Tommy sent Jimmy a magic kit for Christmas to be a magician. Jimmy wanted to teach Thoth how to come out of a hat. Jimmy and me would put on shows all the time. We would pretend we were Greeks from olden times.

Next to the railroad tracks, beside the parking lot of our house, was a big, tall tower that had electric wires on top, and that had four big cement pillars holding it up. Under it was a pile of bricks that somebody left there from before our dads bought our house. Jimmy and me made sort of a Greek pretend house out of them.

It was really like the pictures in the books Penny had of old Greek places. Like the Greek ruins, there weren't any walls or ceilings, just steps we piled out of bricks going up beside the pillars, and places for rooms. We had beds out of bricks just like in the books, except the books had rocks. Our moms gave us blankets to use, and we had dishes and pots and pans.

Penny had all these books from her father dying, from before when he was a teacher. She read them to us. That was how we got the idea for the Greek place. Jimmy would be the Greek father. I would be the Greek mother. Thoth was the Greek kid. Jimmy got his mom to get a leash, like a dog for Thoth, so that was how Thoth didn't run away.

Penny said Greeks were magicians, too. She said they were the first that did shows and had plays. Jimmy and me pretended we were a Greek tragic family like she said they had. We lived in a house by the sea. A lot of Greeks lived by seas. We pretended the railroad tracks were the sea. Except, we would have to cover our ears when a train went by. When they got past our house coming down or going up to cross the viaduct, they would blow the whistle on account of the crossing on the dinky road, at the end of our long driveway.

I hated the whistles, but tried to make it part of the Greek game, telling Jimmy we could pretend it was a ship. Jimmy said that was dumb. Greeks didn't have ships with horns like trains.

But I hated it, so Jimmy said we could cover our ears and pretend, anyway.

We would pretend we wore long, white robes like they wore. Our moms gave us some white sheets that made it look like robes. I would be a beautiful Greek lady, and have my hair up on my head, wrapped. I would come down the stairs real queen-like, and Jimmy would be at the bottom to take my hand like they did and do the farewell, where the men kissed the ladies. Then he would go off to sea on the ship. When he was gone, I would stay home and take care of Thoth —waiting for him to come back over the sea.

He would go hide behind a pillar of the tower until it was time to come back from the sea trip. Once, a train came and blew its whistle when he was hiding. Jimmy said that if it ever happened again when he was gone, that it would mean that he was shipwrecked, and might not come back.

I said, "No! What will happen to Thoth and me?"

"You'd jus' probably die, too! So then, we'd all be together in Heaven."

CHAPTER SIX

I f we were inside playing, when it was winter, or bad, or too hot out, we liked to play in Jimmy's room. It was bigger than mine and had the two doors: one into the bathroom, and one on the other side of the room that led through the big hall into the living room. It was easy to get into the living room to spy on the adults so we could learn stuff.

In the living room, we would hide behind this brown velvet couch that had a cocktail glass table in front of it. The couch and table were kind of like sitting slanted, next to this large, old bookcase that left a cubby hole between them. The cubby hole was right next to the door into the kitchen. It was big enough for both of us to fit squeezed together. The door was always open, and you could hear perfect everything anybody said in the kitchen.

Pauline's kitchen was where the good stuff was always going on. It was like a meeting place where everybody would come when somebody would need help or when people just wanted to talk. Mom and Pauline always kept the coffee pot on the whole day. The kitchen always smelled real good of cinnamon rolls, or like cake, or brownies. The people who rented the cabins came up to pay their rent, and get things fixed, and talk. Some people who were in the club downstairs, or waitresses, came up after closing, to have breakfast sometimes. And our relatives, and Pauline and Mom's friends came up to kibitz about their troubles. Our dads were always talking business out there. It was where all the gossip went on. That was why Jimmy and me liked to listen.

We weren't supposed to, though. We always knew too, when they were going to be telling stuff they didn't want us to know about. If we were in the kitchen, they would start giving each other looks and saying things in funny ways, like using code and spelling. We were supposed to go play, so we just started pretending like we didn't want to know anyway. We stayed in Jimmy's room until we heard the buzzer. Then, we could peek out a crack in the bathroom door to see who was coming down the hall.

This buzzer was a good signal because one of us could keep playing, while the other one checked. We took turns. See, if you wanted to come into our house, you had to go into this little entrance room off the parking lot, and push a button, and then talk into a box. Pauline, or Mom, or our dads, would do a buzzer for you if they knew you.

People had to use this buzzer to get in. It would let the door unlock, or else it wouldn't open up. Even Jimmy and me used it when we wanted to come in from playing. You had to say who you were first. Dad said it was to keep the riff-raff out. Jimmy said it was probably to keep the robbers out, or the police out. My dad said they were the same thing, the police, and robbers— at least, some of the police were. He said they were on the take. Jimmy said, being on the take meant they were taking what was against the law. Big Jim called it graft.

Pauline would open the kitchen door in the morning at

breakfast, so once you were buzzed, you could just come up the stairs and walk right in. She would leave it open until after supper, and sometimes real late at night in the summer. The bathroom door on the other side of the hall would be just cracked open.

So that's what we did when the buzzer rang. If it was someone we wanted to hear about, whoever was looking, would run back to the bedroom until we had been checked on first. If it was somebody our moms really didn't want us to hear, they would come to check to see if we were playing. They knew we were curious, so before we got smarter, they'd catch us hanging around the kitchen all the time trying to listen. After we got smart, we would just pretend to be playing in Jimmy's room.

After Mom or Pauline would stick their head around the door into the bedroom from the bathroom, we would sneak out of the other door in Jimmy's room, and crawl on our stomachs real quiet, and listen from our hiding spot in the living room.

Boy, were grownups weird! They were always tattling on each other. And changing everything around when they would go telling it, and making everything sound different like it would come out better for them. Like it wasn't their fault. Sometimes, they would believe it had been the way it wasn't. Like they would forget how it had really been—sort of like, if you were lying, but not meaning to. It would be like playing a trick on yourself.

Big Jim explained it like somebody had been kidding himself. He said that if you could play a trick on yourself, you could play a trick on somebody else, and then you'd think you wouldn't get blamed. So how could you be bad if you really had been tricked by your own self? He said that was how people acted. They tricked themselves into believing stuff that wasn't true. Some did anyway.

Bo Bo Rapallo was somebody Jimmy's dad said was a trick

player. Big Jim said Bo Bo was always thinking he was some-body he wasn't. Only Bo Bo got "cut down in size" later when all this trouble he got in over the police thing started up.

I liked him a lot, anyhow. My dad said my mom was always liking somebody a lot anyhow, too. Pauline was, too. Forgiving people for their shortcomings too much, my dad said, was what it was about. Pauline said so were Dad and Big Jim, when they all got talking about it once when they didn't know we were listening.

Pauline said, "You guys just don't want to admit it! You are always giving everybody too many chances." I always thought that meant they were kidding themselves, too.

It was dumb Jimmy said, and he was never going to be like that when he grew up. Jimmy got mad at Bo Bo when he got into trouble. He didn't like him so much anymore. Bo Bo got real hurt about it.

One thing was that Bo Bo wasn't phony acting with us like a lot of grownups. It used to drive Pauline crazy.

She was always yelling, "Not in front of the kids!"

She would grab something, usually one of these big wooden spoons she used to cook with, and half-kidding like, pretend to hit him. Only, he would get her by the waist, and start dancing around the kitchen, and she would start laughing. Then, he would grab me and start dancing. Then, he would grab Jimmy and give him a big hug like he said the Italians did. He was Italian.

He was what my mom called, "A real card, all right!"

He used to tell us long, silly stories and give us money. And tease. He was always teasing. Making us guess, "Okay, which hand's the quarter in?" he would say.

I had this big crush on him, starting at about age three. He was movie-star beautiful with this bunch of black, curly hair. Jimmy would get jealous mad at me.

"Betcha he don't really even like ya anyhow!"

"You're jus' bein' mean," I said.

"Am not, he is always getting everybody to fall over him. Mom said so!" Jimmy said.

Pauline was always yelling at Bo Bo on account of his being handsome and all. "Bo Bo, you can't get through life on your looks!"

He just laughed and said, "Bet me!"

It made her crazy nuts. She wouldn't be joking sometimes, either! Once, she started to cry. Pauline wasn't no crier, neither. Bo Bo grabbed her and was trying to talk to her, real soft like.

"C'mon honey, nothing's gonna happen," he said.

She shoved him away. "Listen to me, you're playing with the wrong people, and you're going to wind up in jail, or dead, if you're not careful!" she said, trying not to, but starting to cry.

When Pauline started bawling, though, we knew it had to be bad. She was pretty fast about laughing, but never crying. It was embarrassing to have everybody staring at you. My mom was the same way. So if there was anything Jimmy and me couldn't stand, it was to see them bawling.

When she saw us watching, she gave Bo Bo a look, like I knew was a signal, and she went out of the room. Bo Bo started messing around with us, asking Jimmy questions about movies and a cowboy show we liked. When she came back, she wasn't crying anymore and pretended like nothing happened.

Jimmy and I knew what it was about. We had heard Big Jim talking about Bo Bo, and saying how he was worried, all right. It was over Bo Bo doing something he wasn't supposed to be doing. Only, we didn't know what being a bookie meant—or skimming off the top.

And we didn't know that it meant something that happened later would be that bad!

CHAPTER SEVEN

Jimmy and I didn't cry much, but I wasn't as good at holding it in as Jimmy. Only sissies cried unless it was something really bad, then it would be okay. Only, you had to do it quiet and nice like the way our moms did it. That was the hard part.

That is part of how come Petey was always driving us nuts, always blubbering all over the place, being a bawl baby.

Petey was this kid that belonged to these people named Berry. They moved into one of the cabins our dads' rented, in June the year we were going to be six, and Petey was going to be five. He was pretty small for his age, though. He was more like three. Jimmy was always calling him baby when he wasn't calling him something more worse. It was because he was always peeing his pants.

Jimmy called him "Pissy Petey." I mean, like all the time, he was peeing his pants, and his mom, Selma, would never change them. He would smell like a diaper pail that hadn't been cleaned in about a month.

He was always picking his nose and eating it, or else there would be snot all over his face. He was always whining, too.

Boy, you couldn't even touch him, and he would start whining. Even when his pants were dry, and he wasn't picking his nose, he was still a real mess. His trousers would always be too big. He was always trying to pull them up and tighten his belt, but they'd be dragging on the ground anyway. His shoes were always untied, so he was always tripping over them, then bawling if he fell down. He was always doing it—falling down and bawling. He had hair that was almost white, from the sun in the summer Mom said, but it was always dirty looking, like the rest of him—like old oily, stinky, pee, and creek water.

He always wanted to play with us and trailing us all over the place. His family moved in when it was just getting warm outside. Right away, he got a big hero thing over Jimmy. He started following Jimmy close. Everywhere. All the time. If Jimmy would stop quick, he would run into him.

Petey always wanted to play with our rabbit, Thoth. Once, we caught him pulling on his ears. Thoth had long white ears and beautiful, beautiful, fur-like snow. I thought Jimmy was going to get crazy. Jimmy loved Thoth about more than anything. After that, Jimmy told Petey he better never touch Thoth ever again, or else.

Petey just said, "Okay," sad-like with his head down.

He was always acting like he would do whatever Jimmy wanted. Jimmy could say about anything, and Petey would do it. Jimmy would tell him dumb stuff, I mean really dumb stuff, and Petey would believe it. It would drive Jimmy nuts!

Petey was like that with his dad, too. He was always saying how his dad said all these terrific things, and acting like his dad knew everything, better than about anybody's dad. He was always saying how his dad could do anything that we would be talking about. What was dumb about it was that his dad was always knocking him around and treating him mean.

He wasn't anything like Petey made him out to be. Jimmy said that it was because if it was your dad, that would mean you would have to stand up for him, even if you knew it wasn't true. On account of it being your dad. At least, till you got grown up.

Petey didn't even know it was lies. That is what got Jimmy. Jimmy kept wanting him to see the truth about stuff. That, and then the other things made us really crazy.

One of us would always be yelling at him, "*GOD*, will ya wipe your nose!" "Didja pee again?"

We sometimes used tricks to keep him away from us. He was always waiting down by the door for us to come out in the morning. We would try to sneak out before he got there and go play in the fields past the backyard, where we knew he wasn't allowed to go alone. If he would catch us, we would let him come along, but if he was all really pee smelling, we would get him to play hide-and-seek with him hiding and us seeking. Only, we wouldn't be seeking. It would take him forever to figure out we weren't coming back. He didn't catch on too fast.

One time we left and were gone a long time, but this time he was doing the seeking. Jimmy ran ahead of me, and when I caught up, he was laughing his nutty head off. He grabbed me to be quiet and follow him. When we got closer, we could hear Petey bawling like usual. We peeked around a bush, and there he was, still calling us, thinking we were still hiding.

It wasn't that we were trying to be purposely mean. Most of the time, we would play with him for a while even though we didn't really want to, but we'd feel pretty bad if we didn't treat him good. He didn't have any other kids to play with. And on account of the way his parents were—we found out about the way they were from spying. We were mostly sorry we did.

I told Jimmy that maybe that was why we always felt bad

over Petey when we got mean with him. Maybe, because God was being mean back to us, on account of us always spying and knowing stuff only adults were supposed to know about. Jimmy said God would never do something like that. Only people would be mad and get you back. Our moms said God was just good.

Petey's mom, Selma, was always coming up to talk to my mom or Jimmy's mom about Chappy beating her up. Chappy was Petey's dad. Selma had polio when she was a kid, and still had to wear this ugly metal brace thing on one leg, and she walked all limped and stiff-legged. It was pathetic. She was always having black eyes or beat-up marks.

She was always complaining about her ears hurting, and saying how she wished Chappy would be smarter, so he could get a better job. So they could move away, and not have to live so close to the trains. She said they were what caused her ears to ring.

I heard Mom say once, "Trains my foot, bullshit! From being smacked around so much. It's a wonder her ears don't permanently ring!"

Finally, Chappy beat her up real, real bad, and Pauline said somebody would have to do something. That usually meant the dads. So Jimmy's dad went down and had this talk with Chappy. When he came back up again, he told Pauline that Chappy said he had never meant to hit Selma hard, but that she made him crazy going on about how he was stupid, and a dumb bastard—and how all she did all day was sit on her ass, and read romance magazines—how all she ever made to eat was slop, and how she never took care of Petey right.

Afterward, Selma tried to tell it different. She tried to make it sound like she cooked better and didn't read magazines so much. Only Jimmy and me knew the part about the place being a pig's sty was true. We were just in there once, and it was all we ever wanted to be! When we were, Jimmy and me had been looking at each other, thinking the same thing. The whole place had old magazines and clothes and junk all over. Some of those cabins, like Chappy and Selma's cabin, were always wet feeling. Mom said they were musty because it was from being made out of cement blocks.

That is what made it worse than ever. Jimmy and me were standing there waiting for Petey, but I was thinking if we didn't get out fast, one of us was going to throw up. The whole place smelt like Petey after he had peed his pants four times in a row, without having them changed.

Big Jim said it was just as much Selma's fault as Chappy's. How if she would stop provoking it, Chappy, maybe wouldn't treat her so bad. Only, he said Chappy was wrong, no matter what the reason. A man was never supposed to hit a woman. It was wrong.

Even if Selma was causing it like Big Jim said, I didn't care, and I sure liked Selma better than Chappy. So did Jimmy, but he thought they were both nutty. I mean, how could you not feel sorry for her limping around? Jimmy said she was dumb, though, for marrying Chappy.

Besides, when there was nothing bad going on, she was fun. Most of the time, she was just laughing and kidding a lot. Our moms really liked her. Pauline said a lot of the times she could brain her, but she was the kind of person you still liked anyhow. I guess that was sort of the way I mostly felt about Petey, only not as much. Jimmy didn't feel that way as much as I did. Petey drove him crazier.

That was what finally got us in this big mess that happened when we were older.

CHAPTER EIGHT

Petey made Jimmy almost as crazy as old Ben Beacon did, whose eyes were always watering. Only, it wasn't from bawling. It was from drinking too much whiskey. He wasn't that old either, but he had "a lot of miles," Dad said.

Boy, later on, Jimmy really hated him. At first, before Beacon *took to the bottle* like Bo Bo called it, he was okay. He worked all the time for our dads and didn't ever say much. He was, I guess, pretty handsome with a lot of dark hair with some white going through it. He had nice dark eyes whenever he looked at you, normal. He never looked at people much, though.

Mom said drinking was sort of a sickness for some. She told us some adults couldn't handle it and shouldn't drink at all. Jimmy thought that was what was wrong with Beacon until something horrible happened. After that, Jimmy said something else was wrong with Beacon like he was really nuts. What my dad sometimes called having a screw loose—that kind of nuts.

We were told to stay away from him. He scared me half to

death, especially after he started with the bottle all the time when he would be drunk. If you looked at him too long, he would glare at you with a snarly look. Jimmy would glare right back at him. Jimmy said Beacon wouldn't dare lay a hand on us, or Big Jim would flatten him. Beacon would mostly sleep all day and go boozing all night. We would see him leave if we were out playing later, right as it was getting dark, when we were going inside. He lived in one of those trailers that looked like a silver bullet.

He did this carpentry work one time in the club on the first floor. Right after he got done, when we were spying, we heard our dads talking with Bo Bo about how the club might get busted. Dad made a joke, saying how the big wigs in the police department probably wanted to take a look, now that the club had all these improvements that Beacon did. How they were probably going to charge more now to let our dads stay open. Beacon put in a new dance floor and other stuff he built.

That was when we found out what the police did when they raided was fake. Our dads hid most of the money from the club in our rocking chairs when our dads knew the police were raiding. They just left them a little in the cash register to take. We heard my dad tell Bo Bo that when you read it in the newspapers, it was like going to the movies. You would believe it was real if you didn't know better. Only a lot of the police that raided knew better, on account of they came in the club when they were off duty, and not dressed in police uniform clothes.

So, our dads took most of the money out from the cash register when the police chief told him they were going to raid. They hid it in our rocking chairs. Our rocking chairs were in a place the cops would never look. Jimmy and me had matching rocking chairs in our playroom—well, it was only an attic room, but our moms made it cute. We had tea there with this little china tea set and my mom's cakes. She made lemon cream and German chocolate.

Anyway, when Beacon was working for our dads on the club, Big Jim let Beacon park his trailer right next to the back of our house, kinda tucked in behind the little entrance place off the parking lot, where you got buzzed to come in for the doors to open. Afterward, he just stayed around to do repair jobs.

Bo Bo said, "Jim, when the hell you gonna get rid of that asshole?" Bo Bo didn't like Beacon on account of he didn't trust him. Bo Bo said Beacon had a drinking problem, and it brought out the worst in him, even if the work he did on the club was what Big Jim and Dad said was top notch.

After Big Jim got up to go to the bathroom, Pauline told Bo Bo he could have tried using a little more "finesse." Bo Bo said it wouldn't have done a bit of good. Big Jim had a blind spot when it came to seeing things his own way. Once he made up his mind, that was the end of it. He would have to be proved wrong before he would see it different—if he ever would.

Bo Bo said Big Jim would sit right there, and listen real attentive like to every word you were saying, stare you right in the eye, like he was taking it under consideration, then get up, and never say one more word about it like you had been dismissed. Bo Bo said he would rather Big Jim just tell him to go straight to hell.

One morning, I dared Jimmy to knock on Beacon's trailer door. I did it mostly because Jimmy was always daring me. Besides, I knew he was really scared, though he was always saying how he wasn't, and being a smarty-pants, like he was the one who was always right.

How it started, was that the night before, when it was getting dark, we saw Beacon leaving.

One time in the morning, when we went out to play, we found him all drunken-up and passed out. He looked real sad to me. He was rolled up in a ball, lying close up against the house. He was all covered in grass wet from the dew; on account it had been fresh-cut the day before. He was holding himself like little kids do when they're cold and scared.

When we found him, Jimmy went in and told Pauline. She got Big Jim out of bed to come get Beacon. Big Jim and my dad had a talk with him. We heard our moms discussing it. They were upset with us finding Beacon like that. Pauline said Big Jim and my dad, both talking to Beacon, would surely mean he would really straighten-up like he promised he would. Big Jim told him if he ever caught him drunken-up again, that would be it!

Jimmy didn't believe it would stop Beacon. That was why when we saw Beacon leaving again, Jimmy said he was probably going out to get soused, even though it had been a pretty long while since we saw him do it last.

I said, "Maybe he ain't neither. He mighta stopped!"

"Maybe," Jimmy said, like he didn't really believe he had.

The next morning, Jimmy said, "Betcha, he's still drunk."

"Oh yeah? Betcha you're 'fraid to knock on his door!"

"Bet I ain't!"

So Jimmy beat on the door. Only nothing happened, and Jimmy got really smarty-cock like.

"Aw, he's probably still too drunken-up to come," Jimmy said.

Only, we heard Beacon's footsteps and the lock being undone. I thought we should run, but we didn't.

"Well, lookie here, did ya two just come to pay me a visit now?" Beacon said, smirk looking.

Then Beacon was leading us inside, and I kept thinking how afraid I was, and how we shouldn't be going. Jimmy was scared, too, but he was trying to act like he wasn't.

It was summer out, but Beacon was dressed in this white

winter underwear that was unbuttoned in the front. You could see his muscles and his chest hairs. His hair was matted up looking, and he was whiskery from not shaving. His breath smelled awful like dead rats. Worst was his eyes. They were all bloodshot—sort of like devil eyes.

He was cleaning his guns. He said we could watch. He told us where to sit in this booth like he was making us. I had to sit next to Beacon after he sat down and patted the seat by him for me, and Jimmy was across from us. The table with the guns was in between us. Boy, did I ever want to get out of there!

"You ever been huntin' with your daddy up North boy?"

"Nuh-unh," Jimmy said.

Beacon had all these guns. A big shotgun that he was getting ready to clean and these other guns I saw all over the place. Some were on a chair, and one was on a counter. On top of a table, there was a box open with bullets spilled out.

"You ever killed somethin', boy?" He asked, kind of laughing like it was ugly funny.

"Nuh-unh."

"You kids is always watchin' me, ain't cha? Always thinkin' you're real cute gigglin' at me. Answer me, boy! I said ya was always watchin' me!"

"Nuh-unh."

"Is that all you can say, boy, 'nuh-unh'?"

"No!"

"You're a real brave one, now ain't cha? Well now, let's just see how brave ya are?"

He said, "Come on, hon, bet ya ain't never held no gun before." He called me hon. "Come on now, just run your little paddy over that nice cool metal. Put your little finger right on that trigger. Don't that feel good, huh? Bet ya never aimed a gun at no one neither, huh? Just look right through that sight right there, between the eyes of your little brat friend who's daddy thinks he's such a smart ass big shot."

"We hafta go now," Jimmy said, shoving the gun out of his face, and grabbing my arm.

I was so scared. Jimmy had to drag me off the seat and out of the trailer door, and down the steps. All the time, we could hear old Beacon laughing his real cackle, ugly laugh. Later, after I got over crying and being so scared, I said Beacon probably did it because he thought we made fun of him, so to frighten us. Jimmy said no—Beacon was just crazy. Jimmy said he was going to kill somebody yet.

CHAPTER NINE

In summer, there was an extra present for Jimmy. Uncle Tommy found out about him making Thoth his rabbit for his magic act. He sent Jimmy a book with a magician's top hat, a cape, and a wand. He got them in a magic shop in New York for real magicians. Boy, was it neat!

Pauline made Jimmy put everything on, then she made up this card table with a black cloth on it, and she took pictures to send to Uncle Tommy of Jimmy, Thoth, and me. Uncle Tommy sent me this little outfit, so I got to be the assistant for Jimmy. It was real cute and made out of blue satin, with a little blue satin cape that had this high collar, like a princess would wear.

You should have seen the pictures. There was a whole bunch. There was one with Thoth coming out of Jimmy's top hat on the card table—like Jimmy had really made Thoth appear out of nowhere. There was one with Jimmy holding up the black cloth alone. The next one you were supposed to look at, was of me holding Thoth, and Jimmy pointing his wand to mean he made us appear out of the cloth. Jimmy said someday he was really going to learn those tricks. He wanted to learn to do sawing-in-half tricks, with me in a box, and the trick where you could make Thoth appear out of a hat for real. Uncle Tommy was going to send him another book on how to do even more tricks, but then this awful stuff happened.

Jimmy and me were doing what we weren't supposed to be doing to start with. See, we weren't supposed to cross over the train tracks alone.

Mostly, we wouldn't have wanted to neither. There was nothing on the other side anyway, except this big old billboard. But this summer, nobody cut the weedy grass over there like they usually did. Ever since spring, it just kept growing and growing. So that is what got us started on the idea of going over there.

The grass got really tall by July. It was all perfect. You could see it moving when the wind would blow. It was swaying together like a dance. It looked like those pictures you see of the natives when they are hunting lions. When the grass is taller than they are. That was just how much it grew. Jimmy and I figured it must be clear over our heads. It was like some wild place in the movies. Jimmy kept saying, "C'mon, no one'll know!"

I was really scared, though. First off, I hated trains. It was mostly the noise. They were always having to blow their whistles, on account of the dinky road at the end of our driveway. It was right where the trains crossed. They carried all this dirty old coal in the boxcars that were open. Sometimes, the hunks of coal would fall off the top and be laying by the tracks. The dust would go all over the place, and get in your eyes and burn.

My mom had me scared about staying away from the tracks. My mom and Pauline were pretty afraid of them. Jimmy said that was the only reason I was scared. He was always saying I was chicken. So were our moms—a lot chicken.

Anyways, it would upset them bad if they found out we were even messing around too near them. If they found out we ever crossed the tracks, they would probably go nuts! Only, I did really want to go over there. It was like a jungle. We could make a story there.

"I'll hold your hand," Jimmy said.

"Maybe, but only if you promise we'll come right back?"

"Okay, okay! God!"

We were careful and looked both ways. Still, I know it was dumb, but when we were crossing, I had a scary feeling like one of us was going to trip or get our shoelace stuck in one of those railroad logs or something.

So I kept taking these big mother-may-I steps and pulling on Jimmy's hand to follow what I was doing. I kept thinking about people whose cars get stalled, and a train comes, and they get all smashed and die. It happened a lot where we lived, on account of we were a main port for train traffic, my dad said. Jimmy said I was just thinking crazy and imagining stupid stuff.

Boy, it was something when we got over there! It was even better than we thought. The grass was so tall, Jimmy and me couldn't even see over the top of it. We had to keep jumping up to see where the billboard was. Else, we'd get lost. We started to climb the billboard, but I got scared somebody from the house might look out a window and see us.

Jimmy said, "Maybe."

So we stopped. We got this idea to try to build a grass hut. It looked pretty dumb when we got done. Only, for the first time doing it, I guess it wasn't so bad. All it was, was this circle of grass with the insides trampled down flat. When we got done, that got us going, so we started making more like a village. We made paths so you could go from one hut to the other. We made this sort of clearing like they always have in villages where everybody can come meet and have dances and feasts.

We were doing it for a long time and forgot how long. Once you get going pretending, you start forgetting—whether you want to or not. You just start making all this stuff up, and after a while, you don't even know where you are supposed to really be.

Then, one of us would remember and say we better go home. So finally, we made this deal that we would go if we had this elephant stampede first. Well, it was my idea.

Jimmy started kind of snorting, making like elephant noises. I said I would be this native woman with these babies, and he could be this king elephant, trying to stampede us.

Boy, was it funny! He was running every which way. He was going into these huts, and smashing them up, and screaming and screeching, like a whole herd going crazy mad. I just kept moving, and I was running and running. I was screaming with these babies, dragging them along, and staying ahead of where he would smash. We were going fast, and he kept almost catching me. There weren't too many huts left. And then, we started getting closer to the tracks. We were really laughing and all, and kind of all nutty and all, and running, and running, and running. Then he got the last hut. There weren't any left. I had no place to go but up the hill where the tracks were and him chasing.

We were laughing and going real fast, then it was right there, chasing us. Right there. A big, black, freight train. Then things got real funny like. Everything got slowed down like everything was hardly moving, but real clear.

I started turning around behind me, looking, and the train was almost touching Jimmy. It was quiet, too, like there wasn't any noise at all. Jimmy's face looked like something had made it big and close-up. It was just us and the train. There was nothing else nowhere. It was so close-up, I thought we were going to touch it. Jimmy and me split up and I got a real scared feeling. I couldn't see Jimmy and thought we would be all blood splashing everywhere and bones, splattering in bits in the ground, and red dripping all down the train, and smelling like we had been killed—like a fresh-killed animal we found once from a car hitting.

Then we were just standing there together again. It was like somebody had started up the sound—loud. We were still right next to the tracks. Jimmy and me were close together, staring with our eyes and not moving, and the whistle was louder and louder, and the wheels were clicking, clicking, and wind from the train was blowing and blowing in a cloud of coal dust around us, swirling. We kept staring into each other like we were stuck together. We knew we had almost been killed.

We figured that maybe if you were a kid, God made it easy if you were going to die. It wouldn't hurt or nothing. That if you were a kid, you wouldn't be scared neither while it was going on—like we weren't. Only, if you lived you would be scared later. Jimmy said what happened was meant to mean the word that Penny taught us.

It was an omen.

CHAPTER TEN

It was the start of a whole bunch of bad things. One was what happened with Thoth right when the 8:55 was going by. The 8:55 was a morning train. If you lived at our house, you always knew the times of the trains even when you were inside, because they would make the whole house shake. Our moms were always saying, "well, here comes the 8:55" or "the 12:30," or whatever one it was. You could tell by them rattling everything.

This morning, at the time of the 8:55, we were just going out to play. When the train started going by, we found Thoth in his cage, not acting normal. We knew right away; something was the matter. Thoth was just lying there, not running over to us. He looked stiff.

Jimmy was opening the door to Thoth's cage when the whistle started. When it would go off, it was hard to hear. If you wanted to say something, you would have to yell it. Only Jimmy didn't have to yell anything. I just knew. He did anyway. He started screaming. He was trying to get Thoth out of his cage, but his body was frozen. His legs were stuck and wouldn't come out the door. I knew something was horribly wrong. The whistle just kept blowing and blowing. I ran to get our moms. Only, there wasn't anything our moms or our dads could do. Thoth was just dead. He didn't die natural-like either. Big Jim said he got poisoned with the stuff that kills rats. It was on the foam all over his mouth.

After our dads got Thoth out of the cage, Jimmy just held on to him. Jimmy wouldn't let go. Our moms said we had to bury him. Big Jim had to make Jimmy let go by pulling his hands off Thoth. Our moms told us what we were going to do.

Our dads dug a grave way out in the back of the house where our moms had flowerbeds. That is where Thoth got buried. We put him in a box lined with an extra good blanket and covered him with real roses, and we had a real nice, special funeral for him. Our moms read bible prayers about lying down in green pastures and dwelling with God in still waters forever, and the Lord being a shepherd. Our moms said that meant that the Lord loved little animals a lot, and that Thoth would be safe and free of pain with God forever in Heaven.

Afterward, Jimmy said he knew Beacon killed Thoth. Jimmy told his dad Beacon did it! He told his dad that Beacon hated him and me. Jimmy said, especially him, because Beacon knew Jimmy wasn't afraid of him.

What he didn't tell his dad was about Beacon trying to scare us with his guns. Just that Beacon was always giving us ugly looks.

One time, when we had Thoth on his leash, Beacon saw us on the sidewalk, and he said, kind of smirk-like, "Well lookie at the cute little bunny. Really like that rabbit, don't cha kid?"

"Yeah," Jimmy said. "And you leave him alone, too!" Then Jimmy yanked Thoth away so Beacon couldn't touch him with his drunken-up old hands.

Pretty soon after that was when we found Thoth dead.

And after that, when Jimmy and me were outside, Beacon came out of his trailer and told Jimmy he knew Thoth was dead.

"Hear your rabbit died, kid. Too bad." Beacon said, mean like.

Jimmy got crazy and started screaming at him and kicking at him. Beacon just laughed his sick, cackle laugh, and held Jimmy off like he was a puppet toy.

The reason probably that Big Jim didn't believe Beacon killed Thoth, was Jimmy couldn't tell him what Beacon had done to us, or else we could have gotten into trouble. At least, that is what I thought. Jimmy said it didn't matter, anyway. His dad just wanted to see Beacon, like Bo Bo said, "with his blind spot." Jimmy said his dad was being dumb. Jimmy said he even heard his dad tell my dad that it was "against his better judgment" about letting Beacon stay, instead of making him move. I wondered what that could mean, how something could be against what you thought, but you would do it anyway. That is what Penny said when I asked her. I wondered if that was like tricking yourself like Bo Bo did?

Jimmy said our moms and dads were dumb for feeling sorry for people—mostly what he meant was people who were crumb bums like Beacon. Jimmy said our moms were the worst ones. They were always feeling sorry for everybody and saying how somebody couldn't help it. At least, our dads didn't try as much not to make it people's own fault, like they couldn't help it. Mostly, our dads would want to leave people alone, unless it was something big—not step in Mom said.

Pauline got mad at Big Jim when he would want to leave people alone. Sometimes, somebody didn't pay their rent in one of the cabins. If it was somebody new, she would harp on it until Big Jim went down and got them to pay some of the money. Only a lot of the time, they wouldn't pay it again. She would want Big Jim to go back down for another talk, find out what was the matter. One time, he got really mad, and Jimmy and me heard him.

"Dammit, Pauline! Look, can't you get this through your head? Some people can't take care of themselves. They're not bad people, just not very smart, or not rowing with both oars. It's as simple as that. There is no sense in me going down there and listening to another sob story. For God's sake, I've heard them all! We don't need the money. Let it go."

One person we were glad Big Jim felt sorry for was Mona. She lived in one of the bigger cabins that was nicer, like a little cottage house, real cute. Big Jim and my dad did step in over what happened with Mona and her daughter, Alice, and "Two-Bit" Ernie. His name was just Ernie, only Jimmy and I started calling him Two-Bit after we heard Bo Bo call him that once, on account of the fact that he was a two-bit race car driver, and wasn't worth as much on other counts neither, according to just about everybody.

Mona was the only one that liked him, I mean, really liked him. Once, when my mom was pretty fed up with Mona, she said Mona ought to have her head examined, and that Ernie was the poorest excuse of a man she had ever seen. Pauline called him a woman user. Bo Bo called him an asshole. Only, that was what Bo Bo called everybody he thought was a jerk.

Bo Bo couldn't stand Ernie. Bo Bo was always saying something smart to Mona about him whenever Mona and Ernie would be on the outs. That was the only time Bo Bo said anything smart to Mona. Bo Bo really liked Mona. She was real pretty with long dark hair, and big green eyes, and dimples, with a shape like an hourglass they called it. Her being so nuts over Ernie made Bo Bo crazy. Mona liked Bo Bo lots, too. Jimmy heard his mom talking about how they had been lovers, but now they were just friends. Boy, but would Mona ever get mad at Bo Bo when he would start in on old Ernie. One time, they got in a big whopper fight about it.

Mona told Bo Bo that in the first place, he didn't have no right to talk, always going on about what a punk he thought Ernie was, and who the hell did he think he was anyways?

"I suppose you call what you do for a living, *work*, buster? Maybe you just better take a good look in a mirror sometime!" Mona said.

Boy was Bo Bo pissed. He got all red in the face like he might burst open and shook his finger in Mona's face.

"Don't you ever compare me to that asshole sonofabitch, Mona!" he yelled.

Bo Bo went stomping off, and you could hear him slamming the stair door, all the way down on the first floor.

Mona started bawling. Big Jim shook his head, and got up and left the kitchen with my dad, who said he thought he would maybe go do some bookwork.

Then, Jimmy started yanking on my sleeve to go. We were hiding on our stomachs in the living room. I didn't want to go. I wanted to hear the rest of it. Only, Jimmy kept pulling on me, and giving me these looks. Every time we were listening, and anybody got all upset or bawling or something, Jimmy never wanted to stay. He said it was just dumb.

"Jus' when it's gettin' good ya always wanna go!" I said.

"It's just dumb, that's why!"

"Ya just didn't wanna see Mona bawlin' is all!" I said.

"Is not! It's just stupid. It's Mona's own dumb fault anyways," he said.

"Is not! Bo Bo's always pickin' on her 'bout Ernie!"

"So, big deal!" Jimmy said. "She's always saying stuff 'bout dumb Ernie that makes Bo Bo nuts!"

"So, Bo Bo knows she don't mean it. She just says stuff when she's mad at Ernie." I said.

CAROLINE SHANNON DAVENPORT

"She's still askin' for it by tellin' Bo Bo!" Jimmy said.

"So?" I said. "Bo Bo don't hafta start sayin' stuff."

"So, Mona don't neither," Jimmy said.

"So," I said. "How come ya won't listen to the rest?"

"Cause our moms are just gonna start all that stuff they always do. Tellin' Mona how she should kick ol' Two-Bit out. Mona will start defendin' him an bawlin', and my mom and your mom will start feelin' sorry for her and tellin' her not to worry, and how things maybe will get better."

I wanted to go back to hear the part about Bo Bo, but Jimmy wouldn't go back to listen, and I didn't want to go alone. Jimmy said it didn't matter anyway. Bo Bo wouldn't stay mad. Bo Bo had a hot temper, like lots of Italians did. My dad said that Irish people had them, too. Jimmy's dad was Irish. Dad said Jimmy's dad had a different kind of hot temper than Bo Bo's. With Big Jim, it was more serious.

Big Jim hardly ever got mad, but you always knew how it would be worse if he did. But Bo Bo was always getting mad and saying something angry.

Jimmy said it was better to be like his dad, and not show if you were angry, or say what you were really thinking.

I almost always knew what Jimmy was thinking. He hardly ever let anybody else know. Well, our moms, he let know more because you could trust our moms not to get too mad if they didn't like what you were thinking. Except, with stuff we didn't want our dads to know. If you were married, then you had to tell each other everything. I mean, if you got along pretty good, like our moms and dads did, not fighting or anything. Only nobody else, you should do what Big Jim did.

He just listened. He never shot his mouth off like my mom said a lot of men did. My dad was like Big Jim. He listened. Dad talked more, though. He did a lot of explaining about how something was wrong and how it could be made right. Our dads were more quiet than a lot of people. Not the scared kind of quiet, like they were afraid. They just let everybody else do all the talking, and then at the end, they would say how it should be. They were real smart that way.

My mom said people trusted them. Even though that wasn't always a good thing. People relied on our dads too much to fix things, like giving them advice, instead of figuring it out for themselves. Mom said people a lot of times didn't take it anyways. The advice. Like my dad tried to warn Mona about Ernie.

She didn't listen.

CHAPTER ELEVEN

Jimmy was right. Bo Bo never stayed mad. Pretty soon after the fight, Mona and Bo Bo were laughing and joking around, like nothing had ever happened. Except, they didn't talk about Ernie anymore.

Ernie was strange. He was handsome, though. He was what my dad said was wiry, and he was kinda short. He had a big smile, brown eyes, and long eyelashes that my mom said would have made any woman jealous. Not as handsome as Bo Bo, though. And he wasn't as much fun as Bo Bo, either.

Jimmy didn't like Ernie. We sure didn't see what Mona saw in him. I thought Mona stayed with him because he was always around. Bo Bo had never been. Mona told our moms Bo Bo was always running around with other women on her. He even said so. He told her right away he wasn't ready to get hitched. And he sometimes wouldn't come see her for days.

That is why she didn't stay with Bo Bo and was with Ernie instead, Mona said. Also, Mona said it was on account of Ernie not getting into bad trouble with the law, the way Mona was always afraid Bo Bo might. Later, Mom said to Pauline, but not to Mona, that Ernie ran around too—only he lied about it.

Ernie always had this funny way of acting. When he would be talking to somebody, he would stare at them hard, like he wanted them to think he was important. It was almost like he was mad. He hardly ever joked or anything. Not like Bo Bo did. It was as if Ernie kidded around, people wouldn't take him serious.

That was what my dad said that we weren't supposed to hear either. He was talking to Big Jim. He called Ernie a bull-shitter. Dad said Ernie was the kind you could see right through. Not like Bo Bo, Dad said. Bo Bo was the kind that believed his own bullshit. So, people believed him.

It was maybe why nobody believed Ernie. He was always talking. Dad said he was trying to convince himself along with everybody else. Dad said he only talked a good game. Mostly, about racing. When somebody would start talking about something else, he would look away. You could tell he wasn't listening. Jimmy said Ernie never cared about what other people thought. Mona said all he ever cared about was racing. She said that when she was mad at him. Otherwise, she wanted to believe him. Maybe on account of she felt bad for him.

He wasn't a real race car driver. Not according to Big Jim, unless you called stock car racing, real car racing. You couldn't make any money doing it. Most people that did it had regular jobs. They would do it for sport. Not Ernie.

Sometimes he would do odd jobs, but mostly, he just lived off of Mona. She worked as a waitress during the day. At night, she sometimes worked as one, too, and even on weekends. Ernie was always borrowing money off her to go drinking. She was the one that paid for most of everything, even the food. That was mainly how come everyone was always mad at Ernie.

He was always running around acting like a hot-shot race

car driver, while Mona was supporting him. He was always saying how he was going to be a big deal—famous someday.

Big Jim told Pauline that Ernie was nothing but a punk kid, "He's living in a dream world thinking he's going to make it into the big league."

"But I thought you said he had a chance?" Pauline said.

"He did, but he blew it. He won a few races, but he didn't have enough brains to keep his mouth shut. He's made too many damn enemies out at the track."

"Mona says he has friends out there," Pauline said.

"Yeah, flunkies! He hangs around with that Mel character and Russ Watson. Both of them are flunkies. I talked to Dick Wagner, the guy who owns the track. He told me the same thing Bob Gregory told me. Gregory had his eye on Ernie for a while to maybe sponsor him until he asked around. Ernie's a smart mouth. He runs around, cutting everybody else down and bragging about himself."

What Ernie wanted to do was race cars like the kind they do in the Indy 500. A lot of racers started out racing stocks. Only, to get in the big races, you needed a sponsor unless you had a lot of money, and Ernie didn't have any. That was why he asked Big Jim to help him. A lot of times, somebody would ask Big Jim to help them. Big Jim knew a lot of big shots at the race track.

"Sure, I'll help you," he told Ernie. "But under a couple of conditions."

"Yeah, well, what?"

"Well, for one thing, first, I want to see you go out and get a decent job and start supporting Mona the way you should. You know, Ernie, you got a bad attitude. Dick told me you've got some good potential, but you mouth off too much, and run with a bad bunch. You want my help; I'll be glad to give it to you.

You show a little responsibility and I'll see you meet the right people."

"So, you think I run with a bad crowd, do ya?"

"Yeah, Ernie, I do."

"What?" Ernie said. "Because the guys I run with like to have a little fun and ain't willing to kiss every dumb bastard's ass out at the track?"

"Look, Ernie," Big Jim said. "I've heard about the little jokes you call fun. And coming out to the track half-tanked up to race. Nobody's asking you to kiss ass, but you better learn to get along with people. You keep rubbing people the wrong way, and you're not going to race at all."

"Who told you I was tanked up?" Ernie yelled. "That's a damn lie! I had a couple of beers was all. Okay, maybe I did some stuff, all right, but I never had nothin' to do with Murphy's car catching fire. Every damn time something happens out there, I'm the one that gets blamed for it. Bunch of bullshit's what it is! Dick's pissed because I beat his little hot-shit kid three times in a row!"

"I bet you couldn't wait to rub it in, could you? That's just what I'm talking about. Didn't it ever occur to you that the last person to get on the bad side of was Dick Wagner?"

"Yeah, so I could be like all the rest of 'em brown assin' up to him!"

"Well, maybe they do," Big Jim said. "But remember this, it's going to be a lot of those brown asses that find themselves with sponsors, and racing on the circuit!"

"Yeah, well it stinks, that's what!" Ernie said. "Most of those guys are using Wagner, out there buttering up his kid that couldn't race his way out of a paper bag."

"Look, so it stinks. That's the way it is. You want to race cars or do anything else in life; then you better learn to play by the rules."

"So, how am I supposed to work and drive, too?"

"What?" Big Jim said. "You can bartend nights like you were before. You're out half the night anyway!"

"Yeah, well, I'll think about it."

Then, Ernie went out and got all drunken-up, and ran into Big Jim late at night. Big Jim had stepped outside from the club downstairs with a couple of guys he knew, Pauline told Mom, to get some fresh air and talk.

Big Jim said Ernie got mouthy right away by telling him, "I got something to say to you! You ain't no different than the rest of those dirty sonsabitches! I don't need your goddamn help you dirty sonofabitch!"

He started swinging and trying to hit Big Jim, but he fell over instead, and they had to carry him home. The next day, Mona came up to talk to Big Jim. We quick crawled into the living room to hide, so we could hear what would happen next after we heard all the other stuff. Jimmy said he bet Mona was going to try and tell his dad that Ernie was sorry like she was always defending him. Jimmy was right.

"I know he shouldn't have done it," Mona said. "He gets drunk and says things he doesn't mean. I know he's too touchy about things, but he's been shoved around his whole life! When he was a kid, all his dad ever did was beat him up and call him names. He takes things too personal."

"Look, Mona," Big Jim said. "I don't care how Ernie's father treated him. It's time he grew up. He's hardly a kid now. And I don't care to hear any more about it, either. If Ernie's got anything more to say to me, he can come up here sober, like a man, and say it to my face."

Jimmy said Ernie was never going to change. Jimmy said he agreed with his dad, Ernie was one of those kinds of people that would manage to mess up every chance they got. He never did come up and tell Big Jim he was sorry. He acted around Big Jim like nothing happened. Pauline told Mom, Ernie said something to her though, about how he guessed he got pretty messed up, and how he hoped Big Jim wasn't mad at him. Pauline said she talked to Ernie about needing to start changing his ways.

I was always hoping he would change. Mom and Pauline were always hoping he would. They sure liked Mona, and Mona was always hoping he would. Mom said it made her sick why Mona had to pick Ernie in the first place. Pauline said that was probably Mona's only big fault. She had this thing for helpless men—men that needed mothering and taking care of.

Later, that was why Ernie finally left her, too, according to Mom, when Mona couldn't take care of him any longer. Ernie went to live with some other woman when Mona got sick. She got fired from her job, on account of she missed so much work. Alice came up, crying, and told Pauline. Alice was older, like seventeen or something.

"She's been acting funny and getting sick all the time," Alice said. Especially in the morning. But she won't go see a doctor. She lost her job last week. She's sick in bed again this morning. She just told me to go on to school, and she'd be fine, but I'm scared."

Pauline and Mom went down right away, and Pauline hollered up from downstairs to the little window by the kitchen that was open with the screen in, where Jimmy and me were watching.

"Jimmy, get your dad to come to the window, fast!"

So we ran and got Jimmy's dad.

"What's the matter?" Big Jim yelled down to Pauline.

"Jim, call an ambulance, and get down here! And make the kids stay up there!"

The ambulance came wailing loud and scary. These two men dressed in white got out with a bed on wheels. They went in and got Mona and put her in the ambulance. Jimmy and me were watching. Mona hardly looked like Mona. She looked weird and sick. Pauline went in the ambulance with Mona, and Alice and Big Jim followed in the car. My mom came back upstairs to stay with Jimmy and me. My dad wasn't home.

Jimmy said Mona might die. I kept saying no, she wouldn't. Only, I knew it was real serious by the way Mom looked when the ambulance left. Her hands were shaking when she was trying to fix us breakfast. Jimmy kept pestering me to ask her, but I didn't want to know. I was afraid.

That's the thing that I sometimes wished for—that Mom would fib. I mean, once in a while, a little. With Mom, and Pauline too, you always knew, unless they were teasing around or something, that they would tell you the truth. Always, whether you wanted to hear it or not.

Boy, you better not lie either! That was about the best thing you could do if you really wanted to get in trouble. That was why I didn't want to ask her about Mona, but Jimmy kept pestering.

"C'mon."

"Nuh-unh," I said.

"You're jus' scared."

"I'm not. You ask then."

"*GOD*, why do I always hafta ask?" Jimmy said.

Then when we were eating, Jimmy asked, "Margie, is Mona gonna die?"

"Jimmy, I don't know. She's pretty sick. All we can do is hope she'll be okay, and wait and see."

Later, Jimmy and me were talking about it.

"I don't see how God would let somebody as nice as Mona die," I said.

"God don't let people die, dopey. They just die!"

"Well, he could stop 'em from dyin' if he wanted."

"Yeah," Jimmy said. "But he probably don't have time to go

stoppin' everybody from dyin' all the time. Besides, my dad says that when people's time's up, they're supposed to die."

"It ain't fair!" I said. "Poor Mona! It oughta be that dumb Two-Bit that's dyin'."

"Yeah, only our dads said there ain't nothing fair," Jimmy said.

"Well, our moms said sometimes some things are. It's mostly only people that cause things not to be fair!"

"Whataya think'll happen to Alice if Mona dies?" Jimmy asked.

"She ain't gonna die!"

CHAPTER TWELVE

Jimmy said he bet if Mona died, Alice would come live with us, "At least till she gets wedded to somebody again."

Alice got married before, but it wasn't a real marriage. She ran off with some guy, but he left her. Big Jim got it fixed, so she wasn't married no more. Mona made her go back to school, so she could get a job in an office, and wouldn't have to work in a bar, ever, like Mona had to do to make ends meet.

Jimmy and me thought she would probably just get married right away when she got done with school. She was so pretty and had lots of boyfriends. There were always a lot of boys hanging around wanting to take her out. She wouldn't go out with most of them. Jimmy and me were glad too because instead, she'd take us to do things. Pauline and Mom trusted her to take us places. They thought she was responsible.

The only dumb thing she ever did was run off with that kid she met at the store where she worked after school. He took her across the state line where you could get married young. After a while, when they didn't have any money, and he couldn't get a job right away, he left her there. Big Jim called him a little chicken shit and said he ran back home to mommy and daddy when the going got tough.

"Maybe it's the best thing that could have happened to her," Big Jim said. "Maybe it'll straighten her out in the men account. Or else, she'll wind up like her mother."

Outside of that, Alice was really smart. She could do all sorts of things like sew and cook. She did a lot of cooking when Mona worked. She knew how to make this terrific fudge with coconut in it. Jimmy and I drove her nuts with, "Make fudge! Make fudge!" She made these good cookies and cakes, too.

A lot of times, when Mona went to work at night, Alice would come upstairs with us, after she did her homework. She was good in school. She would come up and do what my mom called "kibitz" with us, and Pauline. One time, they cut her hair and gave her a cold wave, a Toni, to make it curly. And it was permanent. She had this beautiful hair. It was like her mom's, dark and wavy.

Jimmy said, "Boy, are they gonna ruin it!"

He said that because most of the time, hair came out kinky like it did for one of the women who was a renter. My aunt said women left the solution on too long. They were all giggling, all trying to read the directions at once. Alice's hair kept popping out of the curlers. But it came out pretty good. It was short and curled, kind of kid curly. Only, I kind of liked it better long. It made her look older or something long, more princess looking, like Snow White.

Jimmy said, "I told ya they were gonna ruin it!"

She still looked just like her mom, though. They both had green eyes with long eyelashes and perfect white skin. Mom said Mona won a beauty contest once. She didn't look old enough to be Alice's mother. Everybody said so. Mona had Alice when she was pretty young. Alice and her looked like sisters. Mona had run off and got married to this guy when she was fifteen, but he was killed in the army, so Alice never knew her dad, on account of him being dead before she was born.

Alice never said much about Ernie, but I didn't think she liked him much. The only thing she ever said was that she wished her mom would find somebody nice to take care of her like she deserved. We all thought that, too. Alice never stayed around their cabin when Ernie was around.

She would come upstairs, and we would all play Chinese checkers or Old Maid. Our moms played with us too. Alice was good at card games, but so was Jimmy. So were our dads. But they played grownup cards. My dad could deal the cards. That is what he did in the club. He was the blackjack dealer.

One night in winter, after Jimmy and me went to bed, Pauline and mom came in and woke us up, real late, to go sledding. Boy, was it terrific! It had already snowed for about three hours—coming down hard. Alice was in the kitchen, talking with our moms when she got the idea to take us sledding while the snow was still fresh. There was a full moon out, and everything was white and sparkly, with stars and moonlight shining on the snow. Alice said it was like God had sprinkled the ground with diamonds.

It was quiet, too. There weren't any cars or trucks going by on the highway out front. So we got this idea, to take our sled to the top of the train tracks, next to the viaduct, and slide down where it was steep. It worked out pretty well at first. Only, the snow-packed down and got icy. We got going so fast. We almost went into the road. Alice was at the bottom and had to help stop our sled. She said it was too dangerous, a car or truck might come along. So we had to quit. We stayed out for a long while and made snow angels and a snowman. The three of us were like blocks of ice when we came inside. But it was worth it.

Pauline said, "God, look at you guys!"

Pauline was always saying, "You guys!" "You guys, stop it!"

"All right, you guys!" But she was mostly always laughing when she was saying it.

That time she said, "All right, you guys, strip!"

We took off our boots and snowsuits in the hall off the kitchen with Pauline and Mom helping. We always had to take wet clothes off in the hall. Boy, was it a mess. There were snow puddles melting everywhere. Pauline said we stayed out too long.

"My God, Margie, look at their hands and feet! All right, all you guys in the kitchen."

Alice stayed, and we had hot chocolate and cookies. We didn't go to bed until way in the morning. We used to do crazy things like that a lot, before we got in school, and found out about how all the other kids had to have bedtime hours like they were babies or something.

Alice took us to the amusement park once. Well, Jimmy's dad and my dad, and Bo Bo took us. Only, Alice and Bo Bo stayed with us most of the time while our dads went somewhere for lunch. We had hot dogs and cotton candy. It smelled so good Bo Bo had some too. Alice went on most of the rides with us, and Bo Bo went on a few. Our dads didn't go on any. They would have looked funny in their suits if they had, especially Big Jim. He was wearing a hat and dark glasses. He wasn't anyone you could imagine going on rides.

One ride, Jimmy and me went on alone. Nobody wanted to go on the Ferris wheel but us. It was a big one and my favorite. Jimmy wasn't too crazy about the idea. He wouldn't say anything, but I knew. He just didn't want me to show him up.

Boy, did I ever get him back for always thinking he was so smart. We got stuck on the very top, and I thought Jimmy was about to have a fit! I started swinging the seat back and forth—and I thought he was going to die!

"Stop it!" He yelled.

"Why? It's fun!" I said. "Are you scared?"

"No! Just stop it!" Jimmy yelled.

"Nuh-unh, not till ya tell me the truth. You're always being a smarty-pants. Always thinkin' you're not scared of nothin'!"

"Okay, okay! Stop it!" Jimmy screamed, looking sick. "I'm scared."

"Why'd ya say you wasn't then?" I asked, feeling bad.

"You know why! I don't wanna look like no dummy!"

"So, I tell you I'm scared sometimes," I said.

"Yeah, but you're a girl. Didja ever hear my dad say he was scared?"

"So, big deal! Ya don't hafta be like him, do ya?" I asked.

"I'm not, I'm gonna be smarter. God, I wish this thing'd get movin'!"

"Ferris wheels always get stuck. Gimme your hand. It'll move soon." I said, as we held on to the bar, putting my hand over his.

CHAPTER THIRTEEN

Alice took us to the zoo, too. We loved the animals and Alice told us all about them as we went through the park. She read all the signs to us about where they came from and how they lived. When we got home we told everybody, Bo Bo was there, and our dads. All in the kitchen talking before suppertime.

Then Bo Bo said this thing about the zoo that we learned was wrong. He made it on account of when our friend, Penny Yarborough, who taught us about the Greeks, and her friend, Jackie Daniel, who everybody called Jake, had first moved in together into one of the cabins before we knew them.

He said, "Goddamn place around here is starting to look more like a zoo every day!"

We found out later it wasn't very nice and what he was talking about was them being lesbians. We thought it was hilarious the way Bo Bo said it because Pauline even started to grin like she couldn't help it, and so did my mom. But we knew they didn't like Bo Bo saying it in front of us. So we left the kitchen.

Jimmy said it was probably true, whatever "lesbians"

meant. It probably meant they were weird somehow and would probably cause trouble. Bo Bo said they would.

"Christ, just what you need, a couple lezzies! Next thing you know, they'll be out hair-pulling in the drive!"

"Look, Jake used to work for Mike down at the tavern. He vouched for her," Big Jim said. "He never had any problems with her."

"I don't care, I still think you're asking for trouble," Bo Bo said.

You could tell Big Jim didn't like Bo Bo saying it, but Bo Bo got away with a lot with Big Jim that other people couldn't have, Mom said. Bo Bo got away with a lot with everyone. Except, Pauline said one day, his luck was going to run out. Not too long after that, it did.

We wanted to know what the word meant, "Mom, what does lezzies mean?" Jimmy asked later.

"Where did you hear that?" Pauline asked, looking perturbed. She didn't know we had been spying.

"Bo Bo said that's what Jake and Penny were," I said.

"Bo Bo told you that? Oh, brother! Well, that is not the proper term. Don't use it! It is lesbians, and what it means is that Jake and Penny like women better than men. In other words, they kind of consider each other like boyfriend and girlfriend."

"Is Jake the boyfriend?" I asked, thinking that was maybe why she always dressed like a guy in men's shirts and jeans, and her hair was so short, and she never wore makeup.

"Yes, and Penny is the girlfriend," Pauline said.

"Yuck!" Jimmy said.

"Well, it's the way some people are, honey," Pauline said. "It doesn't make them bad or anything. They are just different. It's that something goes wrong sometimes in nature. It's not their fault. Jake probably should have been born a man instead of a woman, but she wasn't."

"How come Dad let 'em live here?" Jimmy asked.

"Why wouldn't he? There's nothing wrong with them. Don't go around judging everyone by what you hear. Don't judge a book by its cover. It's what people are like inside that counts."

Mom and Pauline were always saying that. They were always saying how you had to look at whether people were good or bad. That is what they meant by what counts. Jimmy said he didn't see what the difference was, if they were good, if they did something that might turn out bad—like what Bo Bo told Big Jim might happen, with Penny and Jake getting in a fight. Even like Bo Bo, who was doing something wrong, even though he was mostly good. We wondered how you were supposed to tell who was really good? How did you know ahead of time?

"Grownups are always doin' stuff they don't mean to," Jimmy said.

"Not always," I said.

"Yeah? What ya wanna bet Jake and Penny cause trouble even if they don't mean to?"

Still, Jimmy liked them a whole lot, even if he didn't want to at first. Especially after we got to know Penny, and she taught us all about the Greeks, and history, and read to us before we learned how. Jake, too! Jake was a little like my Aunt Betty— Missy Greenburg, that came to see us all the time. Missy Greenburg wasn't her name, but it was the name I made up for her. My aunt was always clowning around, and that is what I mean about Jake. Jake was a character. Only, not as much as my aunt, who was a real character. Jake was pretty funny, though.

If you didn't know Jake or anything, saw her on the street

someplace, at first, you might have a hard time figuring out if she was a man, or a woman, by the way she dressed. She worked in a factory where they didn't care what she wore, Pauline said. Plus, she walked like a man and had muscular arms. You might get confused, because she was pretty in the face like a lady, and had these nice chocolate eyes that could make you want to hug her.

She had big ol' boobs like a grandmother, only perky, Bo Bo said. He called them perky when we were all out in the kitchen after I said they were squishy. Mom hit him with a dish towel cause I guess we weren't supposed to know. But I wondered. Anyway, after a while, once you got to know her, you would forget about all that other man stuff, and then she was just Jake. You would still want to hug her though. And she hugged back.

Besides being a character, she was the sort you knew would always be the kind to stick around if something went wrong. Mom said she was the kind you knew would always help you out. The kind you could count on.

In the middle of a bad storm one time, when the furnace went out, and the furnace room flooded, she went down with Dad, and Big Jim, and Bo Bo, to help bail it out, when they said it was freezing down there—she was like that. Big Jim couldn't get her to take any money for it, either.

She had this old coupe car that she was always working on. Whenever anyone else had car trouble, they would ask her to take a look at it first. In the winter, whenever someone couldn't get their car started, she would always be able to get it going with these cables to her car she knew how to use.

She was pretty good at doing things with her hands. Once, when Pauline said that, Bo Bo said, "I bet she is."

"Real funny, buster!" Pauline said, getting mad.

"Hey, I didn't mean anything by it. You know I like her.

She's a damn upright person. A damn sight better than most people!" Bo Bo said.

"Then, don't say stuff like that," my mom said. "You wouldn't say that about some guy!"

"I guess, I didn't think about it," Bo Bo said, thoughtful like.

Mom said later, that was the problem. Most people didn't think about things. Mom knew Bo Bo would never say anything to hurt Jake. Now that he knew her well, he would defend her all day long if anybody else made a comment like he made.

My dad said that was the trouble. Most people followed along with what they heard.

Big Jim finally let Jake do all the fixing that needed doing on the cabins, and the house, after what happened with Ben Beacon. We had a handyman, besides Jake, helping. His name was Duffy, but he couldn't do much. Our dads kept him because he was old and didn't have any place else to go.

Beacon used to do all the heavy stuff, but the last year Beacon was around, when Jimmy and I started the first grade, he didn't do much of anything except stay boozed, and almost wound up killing us all and himself, too. He would have been a goner if it wasn't for Big Jim.

The sirens woke us up, and then our moms came in to get us into our robes and slippers.

"C'mon honey, hurry," Mom said. "There's nothing to be afraid of, but we have to get out of the house."

"I smell smoke. Where's Jimmy?"

"Pauline's getting him up. Here, put your robe on."

"How come it's all dark?"

"The lights are out. C'mon, hurry."

The fireman came in to help us get out of the house. Mom said the fireman turned the power off as a precaution. We had to go out down the front stairway that wasn't used. It was all piled with holiday stuff. We had to go fast and my mom almost fell. The other part of the house, with the normal stairway, was too close to where Beacon's trailer was burning up on fire. The smoke started hurting our throats when we got outside.

God, it was awful!

Not at first, though, at first, it seemed sort of exciting until we saw the smoke and fire. Then, it got scary. It looked like the whole sky was lit up. Loud bangs started going off, and flames like fireworks, shooting right up towards our house. We had to get away from the house, on account of all the smoke coming out of Beacon's trailer. It was all around the house. We ran and got inside my dad's car that was parked clear at the end of the driveway, so we could be warm because it was cold weather in October like it was winter.

"What happened?" Jimmy asked.

"Ben fell asleep with a cigarette still going and caught the trailer on fire. Your dad pulled him out," Pauline said.

"Where's Dad now?"

"He's still at the hospital with Ben. We don't know how Ben's going to be, but your dad's okay, thank God."

"Where's my dad?" I wanted to know.

"He's at the hospital, too, honey," Mom said.

"Is our house going to burn down?" Jimmy asked.

"God, I hope not!" Pauline said.

Mom and Pauline told us to stay in the car and got out to talk to this fireman that came over.

"Ma'am, I don't know. If the wind would die down, it'd help. We're keeping the roof as wet as we can. But my men can't get any closer with all that live ammunition going off. There must be enough in that trailer to arm half of Fort Hayes!"

When he walked away, Mom asked, "Pauline, is there insurance on the house?"

"No, we couldn't. Not with the place downstairs."

"Oh, God!" Mom said, scared like.

Jimmy rolled the window down the rest of the way and leaned out.

"What's insurance?"

"Jimmy, will you get back in the car!" Pauline said.

We didn't get to find out what insurance was until the next day. We found out, too, that Big Jim had almost got asphyxiated, and got his hands burned pulling Beacon out of the trailer. My dad said when they got Beacon out on the ground, at first, they thought he was dead. He was alive, but burned up pretty bad. He had to stay in the hospital.

Jimmy said, "Too bad he wasn't dead." He didn't mean it; he was mad at dumb Beacon for almost killing us, and for killing Thoth. "I told ya he was gonna do something crazy! Now our dads are gonna have to buy a whole new roof on account of him."

The next morning, Pauline said she was just happy the house didn't catch fire. Mom said the roof just got a little singed and they had been planning on putting on a new one, anyway.

"The main thing is we are back in the house. And everything is going to be fine. It could have been a lot worse!" Pauline said.

"Yeah, but if Dad had gotten rid of Beacon like he should have, it never would've happened," Jimmy said.

"Well, at least everything is okay now," I said.

Only, boy, was Big Jim ever upset, Mom said. And Bo Bo just made it worse. He started in the second he walked in the kitchen when Jimmy and me were getting our coats on to go wait for the school bus.

"I told you to get rid of that asshole!"

Pauline glared at Bo Bo when he said it like she wished he would shut up. You could guess by how quiet Big Jim was, and the look on his face, that he didn't want to talk about it.

Big Jim was sitting at the kitchen table, staring out the window, looking down at the parking lot. It was like he wasn't seeing anything—just daydreaming—when Bo Bo said that about Beacon. Big Jim looked at him and stared him up and down for a second or so, slow like as if he was wondering if Bo Bo had any brain at all. My dad would say that a lot about people not having any brain at all when they were saying something stupid they didn't need to say.

Bo Bo got all red in the face and tried to say he was sorry. Big Jim got up from the table, and sort of brushed him off with his bandaged up hand, like he didn't want to be bothered with Bo Bo. Big Jim turned his back and walked out of the room with Bo Bo standing there looking at the floor like he was feeling crummy.

Only, Jimmy and me didn't think Bo Bo felt nearly as crummy as later on when Big Jim had to go downtown and get him out of the *can*. That's what Bo Bo called the jail. That time, when they got back, Bo Bo looked like he must have felt about the crummiest he ever felt in his whole life.

They came in and sat at the kitchen table while Pauline made coffee and breakfast. Bo Bo had been in jail almost all night, and he didn't shave, and he was all rumpled and whiskery. He looked real scared too, not joking and kidding around like we were used to seeing him.

Nobody in the kitchen said anything for a long while. It was quiet like somebody died. Big Jim said he would see about getting Bo Bo a decent job, so it would look good when they went to trial.

"I think I can get you something out on the docks working for Carl, unloading, or something. Then eventually, they can put you inside on desk work. But you're going to have to stick with it."

Bo Bo kind of nodded, without looking up, like he felt too

ashamed to talk. Pauline put breakfast in front of them. She made eggs, and squeezed fresh oranges for juice, like Big Jim and Bo Bo liked, with crispy bacon.

Nobody said a word while they ate. When they got done, Big Jim told Bo Bo maybe he better go home and get cleaned up.

"Go ahead and take my car and get yourself showered and shaved, and we'll go down to Kerry's this afternoon," he said.

Kerry was Mr. McCory, Big Jim's lawyer.

Bo Bo got up quiet, took the keys off the table, and left. Pauline was doing dishes. When the door slammed downstairs, she turned around from the sink, frightened like, and stared at Big Jim.

"What's going to happen?" she asked.

"It's likely he'll have to go to prison. Kerry can probably put off the trial, but I don't think we can get him off scot-free."

"I see," Pauline said like she was ready to bawl.

"He was warned, I told him he was going to get caught if he kept skimming money off the top, cheating people, somebody was going to turn him in. Cops knew he was a bookie! But he stepped over the line," Big Jim said, staring out the window in the kitchen that looked down into the parking lot, and shaking his head like he wished Bo Bo had only listened.

He got up like he was real tired, Mom always called it "world-weary," and told Pauline he was going to rest, and to wake him up when Bo Bo got back. Then, that was all we heard about it for a while.

CHAPTER FOURTEEN

I forgot to tell what happened to Mona after she got well and came home from the hospital. We had been scared she was going to die, but not really. I mean, how can you be scared unless you have ever seen somebody dead? We had never even been to a funeral. Though, once we got older, we started having a lot of them.

When Mona came home, boy was she skinny. The grownups thought she looked terrific. She kept saying how good she felt. Jimmy said he heard his mom say it was more due to Mona's new boyfriend, this Don pharmacy guy Mona met in this elevator at the hospital, than her just getting well.

He turned out to be a pretty nice guy, not like Two-Bit Ernie. His last name was Andrews, and he was married before, but his wife died of cancer she got on her boobs. It was sad. She was young. Don got over it, Mona said. She said that people get over a lot of things when they have to. Pauline said that wasn't necessarily so. Sometimes it just looked like they had.

When Jimmy and me first met this Don guy, we kept staring at him, trying to figure out how come he looked kind of weird. It wasn't that he looked bad. He even had this gray hair that Pauline said made him look distinguished, sort of like Big Jim. He didn't look like Big Jim, though. He had a nice face, not movie star like Bo Bo, but friendly. It was that he had this one glass eye. That was what was weird. He lost the real one when he was in college studying to work in the pharmacy stores, and this chemistry thing blew up. It kept him out of the Army. Mona probably liked that.

He was the thoughtful sort. Mom said he was a gentleman. Whenever he would come to see Mona, he would bring her flowers. He even brought Alice some a couple of times. He was always taking Mona places. He took her to the movies. He took Jimmy and me once. And he took her out to fancy restaurants to eat.

Bo Bo said, "At least he's not a cheap-ass, like asshole Ernie!"

Besides all that, he was always planning trips and things for them to do. He had a cabin he built up North, on this land he owned, and he would take her up there. It was way away from anybody, and on a lake where there were all these animals. They could watch deer that would come up close by his house.

He didn't go hunting or kill anything, and Mona thought that was good. He went fishing, though, but that was okay. Mona liked to fish. Mona said fish weren't animals. It was only animals you couldn't kill. Mona had this sort of weirdness about animals. I mean, she was crazy nuts about them. She even liked bugs. She liked birds too and was always talking to them like they were people.

She would be standing outside, going, "Well, hello there, Mr. Robin. Now, look at you, pretty as can be!"

She could whistle just like them. She would talk to the squirrels and also feed them. She had this one named Esmeralda that would come up and eat right out of her hand. Once,

Jimmy and me fed it. Mom said to hear us out there carrying on you would have thought we were all squirrelly.

Jimmy and me didn't think it was weird, just that it was sort of strange to see a grownup do it. I mean, to be talking to all these animals, right in front of other grownups. Saying things like, "My my, where are you off to today, little ant?" That was what Mona said sometimes, like she was wondering what ants were thinking. Well, I did too, but I didn't say it out loud or let anybody know that's what I was wondering.

Ernie used to tell her all the time that she was as nutty as a fruitcake. Every time he would see an ant, he used to run over and stomp on it, just to drive her crazy. Mom said it proved what a sick mind he had.

Boy, I'll tell you, though, the first time Mona started carrying on over a bird—like usual—right in front of this Don guy, well, Jimmy and me thought that would be the end for sure! Only, Don didn't care at all. He even liked it! After a while, Mona got him to say stuff, too. Not in front of anyone. He was sort of shy and embarrassed easy.

Besides, men aren't supposed to act dumb, but my mom was looking out the window in the hall by Pauline's kitchen and caught him. She jumped back and hid behind the curtain. It was pretty funny! Mom got to laughing so bad that she had to run quick and get to the bathroom.

The window where she caught him was the window that looked down into the courtyard. It was open in the summer with the screen, so you could hear downstairs and outside good. Mom was walking past it when she heard Don outside with Mona. They were standing next to the big tree. Don was talking to this bird that was in the tree. Pauline was in the kitchen with us, and Mom motioned to her to come listen and for us to be quiet.

Don was out there going, "Come here, little birdie, come 'ere," and trying to do singing bird noises.

Mom and Pauline were hiding behind the curtains and giggling and whispering, and Jimmy and me had to stay back. Then, on the count of three, Mom and Pauline started singing loud out the window, "Let's all sing like the birdies sing, tweet - tweet - tweet - tweet - tweet!"

Boy, Don almost died! Pauline and Mom thought it was pretty hysterical. Jimmy and me were laughing pretty good, too, and so was Mona. Don sort of did, but he got all funny acting, we guessed, was on account of him feeling stupid. Mom and Pauline said they were teasing, but they couldn't stop laughing.

Only, nobody was laughing in a couple of days. Not our moms or our dads. Nobody came up for breakfast either, or came up to talk, and it got pretty quiet for a while. In the night, we had a big raid, and the police made a lot of noise that woke Jimmy and me up, and we heard loud voices and doors slamming.

I hid under the covers, scared, with my teddy bear, and Mom came in to check on me. She bent down and held me next to her. She was all warm, and she smelt like roses. She told me not to worry. Everything was going to be alright.

Our dads were mad on account of the police coming upstairs where we lived. Jimmy said his dad said they crossed a line that they never did before, on account of they wanted it to look good in the newspapers, like it was a real raid, instead of fake.

CHAPTER FIFTEEN

Mona meeting Don happened the summer before we started first grade. Right after, in October, was when the house almost burnt down. The day after the fire, Jimmy and me went down to look at what was left of Beacon's trailer, before they hauled it off. It was cold with mist outside, and it made the trailer look like it was steaming. It looked like a melted marshmallow that had been roasted over a bonfire—all charcoal and drippy. Yuck!

We never saw old Beacon after that for a long while. When he got out of the regular hospital, Big Jim paid to have him sent to this other hospital, where they teach drunks not to drink.

When we heard that, Jimmy said to me, "Ha! Betcha it don't work."

I said, "Maybe it could. Else, your dad wouldn't have sent him! *GOD*, he got us nearly killed!"

So anyhow, that is how come Jake started doing all the fixing around the house and cabins. She even wanted to fix the roof, but Big Jim wouldn't let her. He said it would be better if he got some men that did it all the time for a living. He let her do about anything else after that, though, until this big blow-up happened.

The next summer, before we were both supposed to start second grade, at least Jimmy did, I had to stay in first grade on account of I flunked, Jake made Jimmy and me this wooden puppet theater with lights and everything. Our moms thought it was the perfect time before we got too old for kid stuff. We heard them talking about it and saying how they were afraid we were growing up too fast.

Jake was good at making things. Mom said Jake was pretty creative and could have been an artist. She even made the wooden scenery. Mom and Alice made the puppets. So we could put on these shows. My mom and Alice were creative types, too, Pauline said. They could sew and draw and paint. Well, I could, too, but not as good as they could. It turned out terrific!

At night, after it got dark, was when we would have the shows. Pauline, or Mom, or somebody, would hold a flashlight for the spotlight. Pauline and Penny helped us write the plays, and they popped the popcorn. We liked it best when Pauline did the corn. Penny burnt it too much.

Still, she was smart with other things, like writing and numbers. She worked for a bank and had to write all kinds of reports, so she was good with words, and knew how to type-write things. She was teaching me because I liked writing.

On the bad side, she wasn't good at cooking or sewing. Also, she had this way about her that could drive you crazy. Pauline said it was because she tried too hard to please people. She was the shy and nervous sort. Only, we didn't find out what caused it until after Jake and her had this big falling out.

Anyway, she had this annoying habit. If she asked you a question, she would say the question about a hundred times before you had time to answer—like she wanted you to know she was paying attention. Too, she was always pulling at her fingers or playing with her hair. She had this short, curly hair like Shirley Temple, and was small for a grownup. Her hair was blonde, and she would wrap a curl around her finger and tug on it while she talked. Her eyes were gray and kinda sad, I thought, but intense, like Mom said. She talked fast like she was afraid she wouldn't get it all out or might forget something.

Whenever Jimmy and me would go over there, she was always trying to feed us some of her burnt stuff. Boy, was it awful. I never wanted to hurt her feelings. She was trying hard to learn to cook to make Jake happy. It got better, but it took a while.

Jimmy would say to me, "Let's say we ate already."

Only, I'd say, "No, we can't lie! We have to taste it, at least eat a little."

One thing was the place always looked nice. She was clean and fixed everything in their cabin cute. She bought little yellow ruffle curtains, and Jake built all these bookshelves for her books. Penny was a reader.

Before Jimmy and me could read, she used to read to us all the time. It's funny, but whenever she would be reading, she would never seem nervous at all. Mom and Pauline read to us, too, but things like bible stories out of these books they bought that were for kids to learn about Jesus and God. Penny read us what she said were the "classics." She was good at telling stories, and she knew all this stuff by heart—all this stuff about Greeks, Romans, and other earlier gods before bible stuff.

We used some of it in our puppet shows. Everybody came when we gave one. A lot of the renters came. We had it in the courtyard where all the lawn chairs were. Jake set up folding chairs for the audience when a bunch were there. Big Jim and Dad even came a few times. Missy Greenburg, my Aunt Betty, came a lot. Nobody ever figured out how come I called Aunt

Betty, "Missy Greenburg." I've never figured it out either. Only after a while, it seemed like it ought to be her name.

She was always joking around. Even Jimmy thought she was hilarious. She was my favorite aunt. I told her that once, too.

I said, "You're my most bestest favorite aunt in the whole world!"

"Aw, God bless ya, honey," she said and gave me this big hug and kiss.

She did these terrific Donald Duck imitations. She would sound just like him. Sometimes she got us all going like a bunch of laughing ninnies. She would get in the puppet theater and start making the puppets do all sorts of crazy things.

Boy, was she funny! One time, when we went with her to see a movie, they were showing this serious part with all these African natives with spears, and it was quiet, and she said right out loud, "Guess which one's got the Toni perm?" Everybody in the whole place was on the floor laughing their fool heads off!

She didn't mean anything mean by it about coloreds or nothing. She was always poking fun at everybody, mostly about herself. She was always saying how people needed to forget about their troubles and laugh at themselves. She said that laughter was always the best medicine for what ails you.

She was always saying how it was the best medicine for the *gallblutz*. The gallblutz was her word for any kind of sickness. Whenever anybody would be sick, she would say they had the gallblutz. She used to get sick a lot. Once, she had to have her goiter out. She used to get bronchitis. Colds, too! She would never stay home in bed and take care of herself like my mom said she should. She would say it was the gallblutz. Then we would all get to laughing. Then she would start coughing, what Mom called, "hackin' away."

"My God, Betty, listen to that cough. You don't have any business being out. You oughta be home in bed!"

The gallblutz was for any kind of sickness, though. Missy Greenburg said you could get the gallblutz from too much troubles or worries. Laughter was still the best medicine for that, too. She said that if that didn't work, well, then you were just a goner.

She was always a kisser, too. She'd say, "Ah, c'mon give your ol' Aunt Betty, a big smooch." Then, she'd grab you and kiss you all over, making wet kissy noises. Go—KISS, KISS, KISS,—until you were smooched all over the face.

She was young, too, and pretty. Well, not real, real young like Alice. I mean, like Mom and Pauline. Not old like a grandmother. She looked like the movie star, Betty Grable. I'm not kidding either! Everybody said she did. She taught us how to Boogie Woogie and do the Black Bottom.

Mom told her, "You better be careful, Betty, you're gonna break something!" Mom and Pauline were bursting at their sides, laughing. She taught us how to Charleston, too—and do the Hoochie Coochie.

That was the summer also that Jimmy and me decided we wanted to be movie stars when we grew up. I used to pretend that I was this great famous singer. Jimmy would play the piano on the bathtub like a keyboard for me. It was terrific! Only I had a terrible voice. Dad said I was tone-deaf.

We used to do songs like—"When I'm calling YOOOOOOOO! Will you answer TRUUUUUU!"

Pauline and Mom made us stop until after breakfast. Boy, did they ever get p.o.'d when we woke everybody up. That was the summer that Mom and Pauline said they thought they were going crazy.

Uncle Tommy sent Jimmy a full set of drums after Jimmy told him on the phone we were practicing to be movie stars. He sent me a baton and a twirling outfit, and we both got a pair of black tap shoes that were terrific on the hardwood floors in Jimmy's room. Only, those were the last things we got from Uncle Tommy. Something happened that I'll tell later.

Afterward, Aunt Flo sent us stuff, but mostly cards, not presents.

Pauline said that as long as we were going to drive them all nuts, we might as well do it in style, so we got to take lessons at a dance studio. Jimmy and me both took tap lessons. I also took ballet—so I could be a famous ballerina if we didn't get good enough to be like Ginger Rogers and Fred Astaire. In that case, Jimmy would be the magician. I would be his assistant and also a ballerina.

That was part of what got us in the big mess with Petey and Selma. It was because of the movie star business that made it even harder to be nice to Petey. I mean, it's pretty hard to be pretending you are some great movie star with some snot-nose kid following you around everywhere, peeing.

That was what the cause was—Petey wetting for about the umpteenth time. GOD, he did it right in front of us!

We were trying to decide what we wanted to do with the rest of the day that was left until supper. The three of us were standing out by the sidewalk in the yard when Jimmy and me heard this peeing noise. We looked at Petey. It was like somebody put a faucet in his pants. Pee was running out around his shoes into the dirt where the grass was all worn off next to the sidewalk. He kept doing it right while we watched! Jimmy got nuts!

"You asshole!" Jimmy yelled. Jimmy smacked him good, and Petey fell down in the muddy pee water.

Old Petey, naturally, started bawling. He started screaming at the top of his lungs, "You said a bad word! You said a bad word! Just wait'll your dad hears!"

I thought, 'Boy, are we ever gonna get it now!'

Petey went running off, bawling all the way, screaming how he was going to tell on us, with Jimmy yelling after him, "Go ahead and see if I care, asshole!"

Worse, our dads were home! One thing was for sure. They didn't like having any problems with the renters. They expected us to behave and not cause trouble. Our moms were the ones that usually settled all the squabbles, so to keep it quiet and not worry our dads with it.

Jimmy said, not to worry. Selma wouldn't say anything around our dads if Petey told on us.

"She ain't gonna say nothin' 'til they're gone. Just watch."

So we stayed outside and played until right after our dads came down and drove off. We buzzed our moms to be let in and waited by the window upstairs. Sure enough, Selma came out of her cabin, and we heard the buzzer.

Jimmy said, "I told ya! C'mon, let's sneak into the living room, and hear what she tells our moms."

Selma wasn't crying until she got right in the kitchen. Jimmy said he knew it was just to make our moms feel bad. Selma was all upset, saying how Petey had come home bawling because Jimmy beat him up. She told how Chappy was home for lunch when Petey ran in crying, and he got out the strap and beat Petey good, for not standing up for himself, telling Petey he weren't raising no cry baby.

When Selma left, Pauline and Mom told us to come into the kitchen to talk and told us what we already heard. Pauline asked Jimmy if it was true that he hit Petey and pushed him down and called him an asshole? Except, she just said, called him a bad word, not the word.

Jimmy said yes, all except the pushing part. He said he hit Petey. Petey fell down all by himself.

Pauline said she was upset with Jimmy for using words that were bad and for hitting someone that was younger.

"It doesn't matter what Petey did, Jimmy," she said. It only matters how you act. People say and do a lot of things we don't like, but that doesn't give us the right to get back at them. Hit 'em or push 'em, lose our temper. Whatever they did, that was wrong of them. But if we strike back, it makes us no better!"

Pauline asked if Jimmy understood not only that what he did was wrong, but because of what he did, Petey had gotten beaten by Chappy, besides?

I was trying hard not to bawl, and so was Jimmy. I started first, and soon we were both bawling, and Jimmy got mad as a hornet!

"I don't care!" Jimmy yelled between the bawling, "I'm tired of havin' to play with him. All he does is pee and pick his nose. It ain't fair that we're blamed for his crazy, stupid, dad beatin' him, either!"

Jimmy went running for his room with me following. Both of us bawling like dummies. When we got to the bedroom, I went over and looked out the window until we stopped. Jimmy threw darts at a dartboard on the wall for a while.

Only, *brother*, it wasn't over yet. In a little while, Pauline knocked at the door, saying how Mom and her wanted to talk to us some more, and would we please come back to the kitchen. Jimmy and me looked at each other like, *now* what?

What it was, was they decided that we were right, they shouldn't have blamed us for what happened with Petey getting whipped by his dad. They said, they probably shouldn't have all along kept trying to make us feel sorry for Petey, and making us play with him. Only that Jimmy was still wrong for losing his temper and hitting Petey. They said we didn't have to play with Petey anymore unless we wanted.

Boy, what a mess.

Well, we said we wouldn't mind playing with him some of the time, not all, but sometimes, if he didn't wet so much and all. Jimmy said he couldn't help it, but Petey made him want to puke.

Pauline told him he shouldn't say that, "That's terrible! Petey can't help it!"

"How come? It's true. So why can't he help it? You try standin' next to an ol' smelly pee pants!"

"Jimmy!" Pauline yelled, but then, she started sort of grinning like she couldn't hold it in anymore, and then Mom put her head down on her arm to hide her face because she started laughing. Then, Pauline really, really, started laughing. Then, Jimmy and me.

"Margie, what are we going to do?" Pauline said, getting serious again. "We've tried staying out of this long enough. I guess I'm going to have to have a talk with Selma."

Mom was sort of half laughing. "I can't wait to hear this conversation! Well, you're braver than I am."

"Oh, no, I am not," Pauline said, "Because you're gonna be there, too!"

"Oh, brother." Mom said, grinning.

Pauline did most of the talking, though. Mom was there for what Pauline said was moral support. When it was all over, Mom said she had to hand it to Pauline. She sure didn't mince any words.

Boy, she sure didn't either. Jimmy and me heard everything from the living room when Selma came upstairs for coffee the next morning, after Pauline asked Selma to stay after everyone else left. Pauline told Selma straight out that the reason we wouldn't play with Petey was because he wet his pants, and was always dirty, and that it wasn't fair, and that she couldn't blame us, and that Selma needed to start keeping him clean, and washing his hair, and changing his pants and giving him a bath, and that she needed to get him to a doctor, and find out why he wet himself all the time.

On top of it, Big Jim went down and had a talk with Chappy. He told him he never wanted to hear again that he had beat Petey with a strap. He told him that a spanking was one thing, but a beating with a strap was wrong. He said that he didn't care what Chappy thought about minding his own business, as long as Chappy lived on our property, Big Jim would make it his business.

So after that, Selma started taking better care of Petey. Only one time after, did Pauline and Mom have to make Petey come upstairs to give him a bath and wash his hair, and send him home in Jimmy's clean clothes, to remind Selma that she was slipping.

Except, he still peed. Only now, when he did, we were supposed to tell Petey to go home and get his pants changed, or we wouldn't play with him. He didn't do it as much. I guess Selma took him to the doctor, but she wouldn't talk about what the doctor said was the reason he peed. Mom told Pauline it was probably because of all the problems between Selma and Chappy. It only made Jimmy and me feel worse, like we should try harder to like Petey.

CHAPTER SIXTEEN

I flunked the first grade, and Jimmy flunked the second grade. We were finally together in the same room with the same teacher in the third grade. We sat next to each other by the windows. It was always our favorite spot. Well, mine. Later, I thought maybe Jimmy sat there because I liked it best. I wanted to sit where I could look out and see the trees and the clouds, and this place that was past the playground that was like a hidden grove, where I imagined fairies lived.

First, though, came the first grade that I hated the most. Jimmy hated the second the most. That was why he flunked. I flunked first, on account of the teacher saying I wasn't ready for school yet. She said I was too small and couldn't pay attention.

Jimmy said she was full of shit! Boy, did we laugh! Only, nobody else heard us, or else Jimmy would have gotten killed. We were listening to Pauline and Mom talk after they had been to school about us, mostly about me.

"Well, I don't understand it," Mom said. "Mrs. Hardy says Caroline can't read. The kid's always got her face in a book. She can read better than any kid her age."

"I know, I wonder why she thinks that," Pauline said.

I knew why. The teacher, Mrs. Hardy, made us read in front of everyone. I had a hard time saying some of the words, even though I knew what they meant. So I didn't say anything.

"Yeah, I'm curious about that, too," Mom said, considering my teacher, Mrs. Hardy, and Jimmy's teacher, Mrs. Rice. "I'm also curious about what's going on between their two teachers."

"Something is, that's for sure! But you could tell Mrs. Rice didn't want to start anything," Pauline said. "Probably because she's younger and in her second year of teaching. She seems very hesitant to say anything. Except, I can tell she likes Jimmy and Caroline."

"Yeah, I think what probably happened was that Hardy and Rice had it out over the kids before we got there," Mom said.

"I don't think Hardy likes Caroline for her shyness and tendency to daydream," Pauline said.

"I know, I was doing a slow burn," Mom said. "And it wasn't Mrs. Hardy's reasoning. It was her whole attitude."

When I flunked first grade, Mrs. Hardy had been my teacher; but, for the second time around, I kept hoping I would get Mrs. Rice, Jimmy's teacher, that he had for first grade. Only I didn't. I had to go back to Mrs. Hardy again. Jimmy got to go on to second grade, but he had the worst luck with teachers. He got Mrs. Hardy's sister, Mrs. Dibbs.

There were only four teachers in first and in second grade. Mrs. Hardy and Mrs. Dibbs were the ones nobody wanted. The *sisters ugly* Jimmy called them. Mrs. Dibbs nobody liked anything about her at all, except her pets. She only liked the kids who got A's and were snobby. Jimmy said it was because she was a snob, too. Except, more than that—Hardy and Dibbs were teachers who only liked the great students, so they would look good at being teachers, Jimmy thought.

That was why Jimmy flunked. He said he wasn't going to be her dumb pet. He hated her.

Our school was small, and it only went up to the sixth grade, so everybody knew everybody. We all went to recess together and had school plays and assembly together.

Everybody said Dibbs was the second-worst teacher. Then came Hardy. The very worst was this fourth-grade teacher, Bissell. Everybody said she was mean.

Hardy wasn't mean, she was just sort of weird. She wasn't fat, but kind of roly-poly looking, and she wore these housewife dumb dresses that my mom called dumpy looking. My mom told Pauline she wouldn't be caught dead in one of them. Sometimes, Hardy wouldn't wear nylons when it was warm before it got cold in the winter. She would be bare legged with hairs showing when she didn't shave. Her toenails were long and stuck out from her open-toed old lady shoes like witches' toes. She treated kids like she didn't care what you did, as long as you didn't make trouble.

She was kind of like Ernie. She never listened to you when you talked unless you said what she wanted to hear. All the other teachers liked her, though. She was always laughing and kidding with them. She was always out in the hall talking to other teachers and her sister, Dibbs, before school, and at lunch and recess. She was usually standing over by some other teacher's door, talking even after the bell rang.

She never kidded around with any of us kids. I don't think she even liked being a teacher. Only, I didn't mind much. She mostly left me alone. She hardly ever even said anything to me. The only thing she made me do was read out loud like the rest of the kids. She never made me read for long. She would call on somebody else. If you didn't read fast—she would always want someone better.

The only reason I liked first and second grade at all was I

learned how to read. Only, not in front of everyone. Just to myself. I loved reading and learning new words. I loved the sound they made when you said them in your head. You could make them rhyme and play with each other, like hearing music. I liked reading more than anything. The bad part was that I didn't like writing the words, only when I could see them in my head and hear their songs. I hated trying to spell the words out. Sometimes, the letters would be all backward on paper. Not the way I saw them in my mind—when I could see the pictures they made.

Except, the books we had to read at first were dumb. They had dumb stuff in them like, "See Spot Run." Jimmy said they were for kids that didn't know nothing. Jimmy liked learning all the other stuff more than me. He even liked arithmetic. Only, not when he got Dibbs. He said she was always staring at him weird.

One time, when we went to assembly, and everybody else was still getting seated, Jimmy said he saw Dibbs talking to her sister, Hardy. Jimmy said they kept looking first at Jimmy, then over toward me. Jimmy said he knew they talked about us.

They talked about our moms, too. After Jimmy flunked second grade and had to do it over again, when school started, we got called into Mr. Hess's office—he was the principal. It was on the first day. When we were in the cafeteria, Mrs. Rice came up to us and said when we finished eating, we were supposed to go down and see Mr. Hess. He wanted to talk to us.

Actually, Mrs. Rice was supposed to have gone with us to Mr. Hess's office, but we thought she meant for us to go alone. So, we didn't wait for her. When we got there, the first office where Mr. Hess's secretary always was, was empty, and his office door was closed. Mrs. Rogers, his secretary, was still at lunch. Jimmy said he saw her go into the teacher's special cafeteria room with her tray when we were almost done eating. So, we waited for somebody to come out. We could hear them in there talking: Mrs. Hardy, Mrs. Dibbs, Mr. Hess, and my new second-grade teacher, Mrs. Carr.

"Mr. Hess," Mrs. Hardy said. "There's not a thing wrong with those children. Yet, I had Caroline for two years to repeat first grade, and she wasn't much better last year. I had to pass her to second grade! But she acts like she's deaf, dumb, and blind most of the time."

"Jimmy's no better except he's plain defiant," Mrs. Dibbs said. "I've talked to him. It doesn't do any good. He'll sit right there and listen as polite as can be. And keep doing what he wants to do. If you ask me, it's the influence of those parents of theirs. Those people ought to have those kids taken away from them. Raising two kids in the same house with an illegal gambling casino!"

"Now, Mrs. Dibbs, we have no proof of that, and even if we did, it's none of our business," Mr. Hess said. "The children are well taken care of. I've talked to their mothers, and so have you. They've been very candid about the fact that the children have been raised mostly with adults. We're not here to place blame. We're here to help them learn."

"Mr. Hess, don't you think it might help if—" My new teacher, Mrs. Carr started.

Then, Mrs. Rogers, the secretary, walked in the outer office where we were sitting, and heard them, and knew we had been listening. She looked pretty scared, and opened the door into Mr. Hess's office fast, and stuck her head in.

"Did you know Jimmy and Caroline are out here waiting?" she said.

Mrs. Dibbs pulled the door open the rest of the way from Mrs. Rogers and stared at us.

"Where's Mrs. Rice?" She asked us. "How'd you children get down here?"

"Mrs. Rice sent us." Jimmy said, staring right back at her.

Boy, did Dibbs look upset. So did Hardy and Carr. Mr. Hess didn't look happy, either. They knew we heard them talking about us.

Mr. Hess told the teachers, maybe they better go back to their classes, and he would speak with us. Only, he didn't have to talk to Jimmy, anyway. Jimmy's dad already did. Big Jim told him he had to start getting good grades, and he better never flunk again.

Mr. Hess was nice about it and everything. He was a pretty neat principal. He was tall and thin, with white hair on the sides, and wire glasses—what my mom said was distinguished looking. He had a nice friendly face, and he smiled a lot. He talked calm-like and looked at you, understanding like. He liked kids a lot. You could tell.

"We're here to help you, children," he said. "But you must try harder to do better with your studies. We can't force you to learn, but we certainly don't want to have to keep failing you."

"Can't I have Caroline's teacher, Mrs. Carr, instead of Mrs. Dibbs again?" Jimmy asked.

"Well, Jimmy, we have a rule here that if you fail a grade, you have to stay with the same teacher until you pass. But how about this, if you work hard this year and bring up your grades, next year in the third grade, we'll put both of you in the same class together. Caroline, what do you say? Will you do that?"

"Uh-huh."

"Jimmy?"

"Yeah."

"Jimmy, I'm not sure you believe I want to help you, but I do."

Jimmy got all red in the face and wouldn't look at Mr. Hess. It was like Mr. Hess had been reading Jimmy's mind.

"Will you come down and talk to me if you have problems?"

"I guess," Jimmy said, looking at Mr. Hess like he felt pretty dumb.

I liked Mr. Hess. Jimmy did, too.

"Least he's not a phony-baloney like most of 'em," Jimmy said, "'Specially Dibbs. But he probably doesn't really want us to talk to him. He just wants us to stop bothering him."

I thought Mr. Hess meant it. Jimmy was always thinking like that—not trusting people. He was always saying adults were always saying stuff they didn't mean. Mostly, adults wanted to make you think they were nice people. Jimmy believed Mr. Hess more than most grownups. Jimmy was always staring at Mr. Hess when he would come in the classroom or be out in the hall with us. Jimmy was always smiling at him and talking to him when Mr. Hess would say something.

Jimmy started getting good grades, even in Dibbs' class. Only, he drove her crazy—on purpose. He said once he started doing all his homework and printing neat, and getting his numbers good, and passing all his tests with A's and B's that she tried to get friendly. He would just look at her dumb like. He would only answer her when he had to, or else he would stare at her. Boy, he could stare, too!

"She can't stand it 'cause she knows I don't like her," Jimmy said.

"Maybe she feels bad 'cause she treated us bad," I said.

"Are you nuts?" Jimmy said. "Dibbs don't like any kid that's smart not liking her. She doesn't hardly even talk to the kids that are dumb."

"Sometimes, she does!" I said. "She talks to me sometimes."

"Yeah, only because Carr thinks you are cute and nice, and

Mr. Hess watches her! I saw him look over at her when we were in line in the cafeteria, and you dropped your fork, and she was right there. She saw him, too. She was only being nice to you, and picked it up, and smiled and all, just to impress him!"

Jimmy's dad said once that was part of the problem with some people—they were more concerned with trying to impress other people rather than do the right thing. My dad thought the same. My mom said people ought to stick to their own knitting, instead of worrying about what other people thought of them. My mom said what you did was what was important, not how it looked. You were the one that knew if you were a good person or not.

I was sure glad I had Mrs. Carr. I liked her. She was always sweet to me. And she talked to Jimmy nice. She would always say how neatly he was dressed, or something, and about his grades being good.

"I like her all right," Jimmy said. "Only, I don't like that it's like she's always feeling sorry for us. Kind of the way Penny acts around Petey, sad-like, because of the way his parents are."

We never said nothing to our moms or dads about what Dibbs said about the gambling place. Jimmy said we better not.

"How come Dibbs made it sound so bad?" I said.

"You know why. 'Cause it's against the law," Jimmy said.

"If it's against the law, how come out dads give the police money? And what about when the police have raids, and tell our dads first, so they can hide the money from the cash registers in our rocking chairs where the police won't look? So how come they don't put our dads in jail like Bo Bo?"

"Because adults are screwy, that's why!"

I still didn't see how it could be against the law, and our dads not get in trouble. It was like the police were lying. When I asked him, my dad said, laws weren't always fair, sometimes

CAROLINE SHANNON DAVENPORT

they only benefitted certain people. You had to either have connections or money a lot of times.

The thing was, nobody else's dads had jobs like ours. Jimmy and me got to go downstairs, where the club was a few times. I liked it, but later, I wished our dads had regular jobs like other kid's dads did. Jimmy and me would get to have chips, and pretzels, and Cokes, and watch the men wheel in meat, and beer in cases, and stuff when it was delivered. We would get to sit up at this bar and play the jukebox.

There was a terrific dance floor that was polished. My dad danced with me on it once. I stood on his feet, and we twirled. He was a really good dancer. Everybody thought so.

The bar had this big mirror, and lots of bottles of different kinds of drinks, and these red and blue neon lights. There was this big wheel that you could spin, and if it stopped on the number you picked, you would win money. There were slot machines that Jimmy's dad showed us how to work.

Our moms didn't like us being down there, so we never got to stay long. Especially once we started school. They acted like it was something we weren't supposed to know about. If our dads would say anything about it while we were around, our moms would give them looks, like they wished they would shut up in front of us. It was kind of like everybody was supposed to pretend it wasn't there. We knew we weren't supposed to talk about it, either. We never thought much about it until after what Dibbs said.

Right after that was when Bo Bo got sent to the slammer. Everybody was trying to act secret around us about it. Only, we knew what was going on. We heard them talking before about what they were going to say in court, and whether Bo Bo would have to go to jail. Big Jim said he knew Bo Bo would.

One morning before school, Bo Bo came over. Mom came

in while I was dressing and told me to hurry and come down to the kitchen. Bo Bo wanted to talk to Jimmy and me.

I got there first.

"Ooo La La, look at this beautiful little lady! C'mon Caroline, spin around and let your Uncle Bo Bo see that pretty dress!"

He took me by the hand and spun me around. Jimmy came in then.

"How's it going, Jimmy?" Bo Bo said.

"Fine."

"C'mon over here. I want to talk to you two for a minute."

Bo Bo was sort of kneeling down between us at the table where we were sitting. He got real serious and sad looking. He put his arm around me, but Jimmy leaned away from him.

"What?" Jimmy said, not even looking at Bo Bo.

"I have to go away for a while. But I didn't want to leave without saying goodbye. I didn't want you two to think I was going to forget about you."

"Where ya' going?" Jimmy asked, still not looking.

"Well, I'm gonna be gone for a while, Jimmy. But I'll write you letters."

"You're going to jail, ain't ya?" Jimmy said, finally looking up at him, staring at him squinty-eyed and hard.

"Yeah, Jimmy, I'm going to jail," Bo Bo said, reaching out to put his arm around Jimmy.

Jimmy started sort of crying, and so did Bo Bo. Only, Jimmy started trying to push Bo Bo away, but Bo Bo got up and grabbed him around the waist to hold him. Jimmy started shoving and yelling at Bo Bo.

"Why'd ya hafta get put in jail? You're nothing but a crook! I hate ya! I hate ya!" Jimmy kept yelling.

Then Bo Bo was holding us both, and we were all bawling.

Jimmy broke away and ran to his room, and Bo Bo said to Pauline, "Let him go."

After a while, when Bo Bo was still holding me, Mom said, "C'mon honey, let Mom wash your face, or you'll miss the bus."

So, Bo Bo had to leave to go to the court and then on to the slammer. And we had to leave to go to school.

CHAPTER SEVENTEEN

After Bo Bo had to go to jail, more bad things happened. For one thing, Ben Beacon started coming back around. He started dropping in to talk to Big Jim and Dad. He didn't drink anymore. He talked to Jimmy and me when we would see him, but Jimmy said Beacon was still crazy and mean, no matter what anybody thought. He would always be friendly to us if we were in the kitchen when he came over. When our parents were around. He would act differently if he saw us alone.

Jimmy said, "you can tell he sure don't like us none."

One time, we were getting our bikes by the door, and he had to wait until we got them out of the way to get past us to go upstairs. The wheel of mine was stuck next to this plant, and Beacon didn't even help. Jimmy had to put his bike down and come back to help me get it unstuck. Beacon stood there staring at us, strange. He didn't even move. Just glared. Jimmy said he hated Beacon because Beacon was a killer.

When we got back from riding our bikes and playing, only Pauline was in the kitchen.

"What's that creepy Beacon doing over here again?" Jimmy asked.

"His name's not 'creepy Beacon.' He was here to visit," Pauline said.

"I hate him. He killed Thoth. He almost burnt the house down. How come dad's letting him come around again?"

"Jimmy, there was no proof he killed Thoth. He didn't set the fire intentionally. Ben hasn't had anything to drink in a long time. Your dad helped him get a job. He's doing good now," Pauline said.

"You should see the way he looks at Caroline and me. Like he could kill us."

"Lord, Jimmy! Ben's not going to kill anybody. He's worked very hard to change his ways and get on the right path."

"Yeah, well, I bet we shouldn't trust him yet!"

With all the bad things, there was one good thing that happened, though. The winter when we were both in the second grade was when Alice met Tally McMillan. Our moms, Mona, and Missy Greenburg cooked that one up. Our dads were always saying how our moms were always cooking something up. Mostly though, they just meant it in a funny way. My dad said it was because our moms wanted to make people happy. They wanted things to turn out good.

Jimmy said that was why our moms thought that about Beacon, too, thinking he had changed his ways, cause they wanted it to turn out good. Jimmy said he thought what Bo Bo told us one time was the problem. "They just wanna think Beacon has changed like Bo Bo said about people when they fool ya', cause you wanna believe 'em." Jimmy said he thought Bo Bo was right about seein' the truth. You had to forget what you wanted in order to see something for real like it really was. If you wanted something bad enough it would get in the way of seeing it like it was, like our moms not seeing Beacon really was a creep. Bo Bo said that was what got people into trouble. Only, Jimmy said, "too bad Bo Bo didn't take his own advice."

I asked my dad about it, he said most people didn't. I guessed dad and Jimmy were probably right. But I sure hoped just because I wanted everything to turn out good with the scheme everybody was cooking up for Alice, nothing would go wrong.

When the club closed downstairs on weekends, Pauline and Mom would make giant breakfasts for whoever came up. On weekdays, while Jimmy and me were having our breakfast, it would mostly be who my dad referred to as "the girls," meaning Mom, Pauline, usually Missy Greenburg, and woman friends. They would be having coffee with coffee cake or donuts and rolls if someone baked or brought something. Once in a while, Big Jim, or Dad, or some other guy would be there at first, but they would leave, and it would be all women.

One Monday, when it was Mom, Pauline, Mona, and Missy Greenburg, Mona started talking about this guy named Tally, who had been in the club on Saturday night, saying what a doll he was, and how it would be great if he could meet Alice. Alice couldn't get in the club yet, because you had to be eighteen, and she wasn't going to be eighteen yet for another month.

"Come next Saturday, why don't you ask Jim to invite Tally up here for breakfast after the club closes, and we'll make sure Alice is up here, too," Pauline said.

"Great idea!" Mona said.

"Who's Tally?" Jimmy piped up.

"Don't you guys have something to do?" Pauline asked, seeing we were done eating, even though it wasn't time to go down to get the school bus. She would always ask that when she wanted us to leave and quit bugging them.

"Nuh-uh," I said.

"C'mon!" Jimmy said, starting for his room, motioning me to follow him. "They always make us leave at the good parts."

"Okay, you can stay, but you've got to keep those little mouths shut about this. No telling Alice what we're up to!" Pauline said, waving her finger to make the point.

"So, who's Tally?" I asked.

"You know McMillan Barrow Company across the street?" Pauline said.

"Yeah."

"Well, Tally McMillan owns that," Mom said.

"God, he must be old," Jimmy said.

"No, he's not. He's probably only a few years older than Alice, probably in his twenties. His father was killed in a car accident two years ago and left him the company."

"Yeah, but what if she doesn't like him?" Jimmy said.

"She'll like him!" Mom said, sure of it.

Missy Greenburg started singing some silly song about how love is blooming, and rolling her eyeballs around, and getting everybody laughing.

Tally turned out to be really cute, like Mona said he was. He was about taller than anyone we ever knew in our whole lives, even taller than Jimmy's dad and my dad. He had dark hair and blue eyes. And dimples when he smiled. And he winked a lot. And boy, Mona was right. Alice liked him.

When we got up on Saturday, they were out in the kitchen having breakfast, and Alice was sitting right next to Tally. Breakfast was almost my favorite time. Pauline and mom always made lots of bacon and French toast, and it smelled so good. We liked Tally right off. He shook hands with Jimmy.

"Hi ya, son. And who is this?" He said, looking at me standing behind Jimmy.

"Caroline, this is Tally," Alice said, with a big smile.

"Well, hello there, Caroline," he said. "Alice has been

telling me about you two. How about pulling a chair up here, next to us, and having some breakfast?"

"Hi," I said, thinking he was nice.

Tally was fun. He treated us like regular people, none of that kid stuff. He sure was a tease, though. He teased with everybody, even grownups. He told Alice that some eggs had six yolks in them! He said he knew. He used to live on a farm when he was a kid, and he had to collect the eggs.

Alice said, "Oh, c'mon!" Starting to laugh.

"No, really!" Tally said.

He said you could tell by the size of the chickens. The bigger the chicken, the more yolks in the egg. He said most chickens were regular size, so that was why you didn't get many eggs with more than one, or maybe, two yolks. Only, if you got a really big ol' hen, then boy, look out!

Alice almost started to believe him. He talked real convincing, but everybody had these grins on their faces like they knew it was a joke, but didn't want to laugh until Alice got it.

Tally was always telling stories. After you got to know him, then you knew it was his way of teasing. He would make up these dumb things and start telling about them. Most of the time, he would be laughing, so you would know he was kidding, but sometimes, he would look serious to try and fool you. Every once in a while, he would get you to believe him. A few times, Jimmy and I fell for it. Once, he told Jimmy that the reason it rained was to keep the clouds white. He said it was a scientific fact. Otherwise, if it didn't rain, the sky would get darker and darker until it was night outside all the time.

Jimmy didn't believe Tally after he went on and on, only at the beginning when he talked serious and using science. Once he knew he had you starting to be convinced that maybe this time part of it might be true—then he would start to grin.

Jimmy got an idea to get him back for all his dumb jokes.

Tally and Alice were sitting out on the glider in the backyard after they started liking each other. They were sitting close, and Tally kept kind of kissing Alice a little, but not much because we were there.

It was starting to get dark, but in the summer, Jimmy and I could stay out till about 9:00 or 10:00 o'clock as long as we stayed close to the house. We were playing Monopoly on a lawn table. It was almost getting too dark to see, but we didn't want to go inside.

"Want to go get some grapes?" Jimmy said.

"Yeah."

Out behind where the cabins ended, on the other side of our dinky back street, there were rows and rows of grape vines and fruit trees, owned by some people that lived in a big farm-house. One time, when we were there, the man was out in his yard. He told us we could come over and take fruit and grapes if we wanted, as long as we only took enough to eat and didn't waste any.

When we got there and got some grapes, we decided to stay there to eat them. We knew Tally and Alice wanted to be alone. Besides, we liked to be in the orchard, especially at night. There weren't any lights, and you could see the stars good, and the fireflies. We would sit under one of the fruit trees for a long time and be quiet. We could hear all the night bug sounds of crickets and katydids, and once in a while, see a rabbit.

By the time we started back, it was totally dark, and that's what gave Jimmy the idea.

"Let's sneak up on Alice and Tally and scare 'em."

"No! Alice'll get frightened," I said.

"Aw c'mon, she won't either. Not with Tally there."

"You do it then!"

"Okay, but you gotta come with me."

So we crawled on our hands and knees, around the back of

the glider. When Jimmy got right up next to it, by Alice's feet, he started making these sounds, almost in a whisper, that were like buzzing sounds. He could make buzzing sounds so good you would think it was a real bug. Tally and Alice were doing all this kissing. We could hear them. They never even guessed we were there.

Jimmy reached up and kind of tickled Alice's ankle with a piece of grass. She kicked her foot like she was trying to get rid of whatever it was. So Jimmy did it a couple more times. She kept kicking. Then, he reached up and grabbed her around the ankle.

Boy, did she scream! She jumped right out of the glider. Jimmy was laughing so hard he was pounding the ground. Tally and Alice started chasing us. Tally got Jimmy and Alice got me. They held us down, and Tally sat on Jimmy while they were thinking up things to do to us.

"Let's turn the hose on them," Tally said.

Instead, they tickled us until we couldn't stand it no more.

It was fun being around Tally. Everybody liked him. My dad said he was the best-natured person he had ever met. Dad said Tally was a hard worker and was really making something of himself. Our parents were talking about it one night at dinner. They thought it was serious with Alice.

"What's serious," Jimmy said, "like they're gonna get married?"

"They might, but don't you kids say anything, especially to Alice."

"Can we go to the wedding?" I asked.

"Tally hasn't proposed yet," Mom said.

"So, why do you think he's gonna?" Jimmy asked.

"None of your business," Pauline said. "We just do."

Only, after we pestered her, my mom said later the reason that they knew he would, was because Tally had talked to

Mona first, being her mom and all, to see if it would be okay with her before Tally asked Alice to marry him. After a while went by, we started thinking he was never going to ask her. I wished he would hurry up. Mom said some things take time. You had to learn to be patient in life. He never asked her until we went back to school to start the third grade in September.

It was romantic how he did it. He took her out to dinner. He told her he was ordering something for a special occasion. He had the waitress put her engagement ring in a glass of champagne. He said at first he was afraid she was going to drink it. She didn't see the ring right away, but when she did, she started crying.

The next day, they came up to tell us. Alice was wearing the ring. It was so pretty with all these diamonds. I got to try it on.

Big Jim came into the kitchen to see it. "You two set the date yet?" he asked.

"Alice wants to be married at Christmas time, so I guess that's when it'll be," Tally said.

"Well, I've got something I'd like to say to you. How about coming into the study for a minute?" Big Jim said.

When they left the room, Jimmy said, "What's dad want to talk to them about?"

"Your dad's going to give them their wedding reception as a gift," Pauline said.

They were going to have a big wedding. Alice was going to turn Catholic for Tally, so they would be the same religion and raise their kids the same. They both wanted a lot of kids. Tally never had any brothers or sisters. His mother was kind of sickly. Alice never had any either. They both wished they could have had big families to grow up in. So they wanted more than one kid to never be alone like they were.

Alice had to go to the church every week to take instructions from the priest. She could be Catholic then. She and Tally started going to church on Sunday. Jimmy and me got to go along. We had never been to church before. I liked it a lot, but Jimmy didn't like it so much. I liked it because the church was beautiful. Everything was like it would be for kings and queens.

It was the way I had seen it in pictures and the way it was described when I first learned how to read. Penny started letting me borrow her books, even before I could read all the words. History was Penny's favorite, and that was why she had a lot of books about royalty and medieval times.

The church was huge like a castle, and the ceiling went on and on like it could touch the sky where Heaven was. The windows had scenes on them of saints with angels and animals. I liked the way the priests dressed. They seemed so holy. The music and singing was beautiful. Everything was said in a foreign language, Latin. I thought it was all very regal, like Penny taught me some things were. It was like being in a place where only goodness was and where God would come to visit if he came to earth, but Jimmy said he felt dumb. We had to kneel at certain times, and pray, and say Latin after the priest.

"So watch what everybody does and just move your lips," I said.

"But I don't like doing it," Jimmy said. "I don't know what they're saying!"

"They're saying mostly prayers," I said.

"Yeah, but it feels weird. Dad says he doesn't go to church because he likes to pray in private. Anyhow, you like it 'cause it's pretty."

"Nuh-uh!" I said.

"What then?"

"It is holy. I know God is there. It's like I can feel him." I said.

"Maybe, but I think it's kinda phony," Jimmy said. "My dad said you can pray anywhere. God will hear you. It doesn't have to be in a church."

Jimmy wouldn't go after that, so neither did I. He didn't want to be in the wedding either, except that he didn't want to hurt Alice's feelings. Jimmy said we were too old, but Alice still wanted me to be the flower girl and Jimmy to be the ring bearer. She told Pauline and Mom we were the only family she had. So Jimmy couldn't say no.

Especially after the fight Alice and Mona got in about it. Mona wanted Alice to invite all their relatives to the wedding and have her cousins' kids, who were younger, as flower girl and ring bearer, but Alice wouldn't do it. Alice came up crying to Pauline and Mom over it.

"I don't care what she says. I won't do it!" Alice said. "I've never even met half of those people. She says I'm ashamed of them."

"Are you honey?" Mom asked.

"Yeah, I am, and I don't want them at my wedding. You should see some of them. My mom's older sister has been married four times, dresses like a slob, and keeps her house filthy. My Uncle Jeff has never had a job in his life that he could keep. He argues and fights with everyone! My mom would never ever go over there before. Now, all of a sudden, I'm supposed to invite them to the wedding."

"Boy, I don't know," Pauline said, looking concerned.

"Mom says she's going to call the priest and tell him what a hypocrite I am. I won't even invite my own family to the wedding."

"Oh, she's not going to do that!" Mom said.

"God, I'd die if they came! They'd probably get drunk and make a scene.

"Oh, now," Mom said.

"You don't know what they're like. Once, when I was small, we went on a family picnic with some of them. My mom's cousin got in a fight with her husband right at the picnic table. They were cursing and screaming at each other right in front of everybody!"

"Why don't you let me see if I can talk to your mother. Don't say anything more about it. It's not going to do any good to argue," Pauline said.

That didn't work. Later, Pauline and Mom tried to talk to Mona about it, but she wouldn't listen.

"I know you've been good about a lot of things, but I don't want to talk about this," Mona said. "Alice knows how I feel, and there is nothing that is going to change my mind. Now that she's marrying Tally, she's started acting all hoity-toity, and I don't like it!"

Jimmy thought it was really Mona bein' that way 'bout wanting Alice to invite their relatives, like Mona wanting to show off Tally's family to them. I didn't wanna think that was it.

At supper that night, my dad wondered if that might be it too, Mona wanting to prove to their family what a great "catch" Alice made with Tally. Jimmy's dad said maybe the reason Mona was acting like she was jealous. I didn't wanna think that either.

"Oh, I don't think so. How can you say that? Mona's always wanted Alice to have the best," Pauline said.

"That doesn't seem like Mona," Mom said. "Besides, look at her and Don. It is not like she couldn't have what her daughter has. Having a great husband like Tally will make. Don is not exactly a slouch. I know he would marry Mona in a minute if she'd agree!"

Only right after that, Mona did the worst thing. She started seeing Two-Bit Ernie again.

CHAPTER EIGHTEEN

Mona started seeing Ernie after I broke my ankle. Right before Halloween, it got crushed under the seat of the merry-go-round at school. I broke it because the kids had it swinging back and forth, like a swing, instead of pushing it around in a circle the way it was supposed to go. When the teacher wasn't looking though, everybody pushed it hard to make it swing up and down and stood on the seats instead of sitting. It was more fun. One side would go up high. The bad part was that when it came back down, it weighed a lot and was low to the cement underneath. It was made to be only high enough off the ground for small kids, so you could push it around, and then sit down quick.

It had rained that day, and I was the last one outside at recess. It was already going high, so everybody yelled, "Jump!" When I jumped, I grabbed onto the seat with my hands and arms, instead of jumping up on top of the seat to stand on it. My feet slipped on the wet cement, and I couldn't pull myself up on top fast enough. The merry-go-round came back down on my one knee. It was bent under the seat where there wasn't enough room to fit.

Somebody had to run and get the teacher. I was screaming and rolling on the ground. Mrs. Hardy came down. She was mad because we weren't supposed to make the merry-go-round swing. Jimmy said that wasn't it! It was she was scared she would get into trouble. She was the playground teacher that day. She was inside talking. Not outside, where she was supposed to be, watching everybody.

She tried to make me walk up the stairs, but I couldn't. So I hopped, and I had to take one step at a time with her helping me. She told me to quit crying, but I couldn't help it. When we got upstairs to the nurse's room, she left me there on this bed, while she went and got my teacher, Mrs. King.

Mrs. King was the third-grade teacher that Jimmy and me liked the best. We got to be in her class together like Mr. Hess said we would.

When they got back, Mrs. King told Mrs. Hardy to go call my mom and dad, and she would stay with me. While we waited for my parents to come and get me, Mrs. King was nice. She didn't yell at me the way Hardy had.

Hardy said she thought my leg was sprained, but I couldn't walk. When my dad came, he had to carry me down to the car. My mom told Pauline later that it was all my dad could do not to tell Hardy what he thought of her stupid assessment. Jimmy heard them talking. Jimmy said he was mad on account of what he said was negligence. When Dad took me to the hospital, the doctor said my ankle was broken badly, because the ankle part was splintered all up inside. I had to have an operation where they gave me gas. I went to sleep and never knew anything. Except, I woke up sick.

When I woke up, I had this cast on all the way up my whole leg to the top, so I couldn't even bend my knee. Only the toes they left out. They were all black and blue and puffy. It was awful. I was pretty scared. I wanted to go home. I had to stay there for five days.

The good thing was that Jimmy sent me this pretty flower in this cute vase. And a card with hearts to get well quick. He couldn't come up to see me. They wouldn't let kids in. There was also this wonderful, nice nurse that washed my hair after I got sick from the gas. She braided my hair and talked to me the whole time, telling me not to be afraid and that my parents would come soon, and my leg would heal as good as new, and everything would be all right. She sang to me and fed me my lunch, some soup, and a lot of vanilla ice cream that made me feel better. She was like an angel.

Even after I got home from the hospital, I couldn't go to school. Mrs. King had to come to the house a couple of times until Mom helped me with my lessons. I wished I never had to go back to school. Even with Mrs. King, I didn't like school. When she came to the house, she started asking me a lot of questions when she saw all the books in my room.

"Caroline, do you read these books?"

"Some of them," I said, kind of scared, wondering why she was asking, and a little worried she might want to take them away.

"Which ones?"

So I showed her mostly only the ones that were easy to read. Jimmy said I never should have let her know that I could read so well. Jimmy didn't think you should tell anybody anything. Only people you could trust like our moms and dads and us. He always thought I said too much.

I didn't tell her everything. She wanted to know why I didn't like school. I told her I didn't like it was all. I never told her the reason, or else she probably would have tried to get me to get better grades. Jimmy thought I should get better grades anyway. If you did, the teachers would leave you alone.

I didn't see why. I wasn't going to need to know most of the silly stuff you had to learn in school. Except, I wished I could spell better. I had trouble with reading right at first, but Penny helped me sound everything out. She kept helping me until it got easy. After a while, I never even saw the words. I could read fast. Only, I could sometimes not remember how words were spelled. Even dumb, simple ones would fly right out of my head whenever I went to write them down. Then also, sometimes I couldn't remember how to say them. Penny told me maybe I needed to have other ones that meant the same, in case I couldn't remember the one I had wanted to say. So she helped me learn a lot of different words. We played word games so I would get better. Jimmy helped me too. It was hard, but it didn't matter. I already made up my mind that I wanted to be a writer.

Nobody else knew about it, except for Jimmy and Penny. I never even told Mom or Pauline. That was the reason I hated school. My favorite thing was reading, but not the silly kid stories they made you read in school. I liked to make up my own stories. When I had to be in school, I was supposed to pay attention to the teacher and stop thinking up things. Except that I didn't.

Even if Jimmy got better grades, I still had more friends. Jimmy only had two friends: Lester and Robert. They were smart like Jimmy and got all the A's. They played card games and word games at recess that were kind of like Monopoly, but you had to be really smart to play.

Otherwise, if Jimmy wasn't with them or me, he would be off by himself. He would never play with anyone else. After the second grade that he had to do over, he wouldn't play on the monkey bars or swings anymore. Mostly, no one did in the third grade. Just once in a while, but he never would. He wouldn't play games like a bunch of us would in the school parking lot at noon recess. We played jump rope, where two or three kids jumped at once, and everyone took turns in a big group. Or else, we would play jacks or marbles, and sometimes hopscotch. I used to try to get him to play with us, but he wouldn't. He would get mad at me for pestering him.

"How come?"

"Because I don't want to, that's how come!"

He would never say why, but I knew why. He was afraid he would look dumb in front of all the kids if he tripped playing games or else lost a lot. Boy, did he hate losing, but he hardly ever did.

I was scared, too, but I liked being around everyone and watching. I would pretend like I was playing. If we were playing rope, I would be the one who held one of the ends for everyone else to jump. Most of the time, I would watch the other kids, like if they were playing marbles. I tried to tell Jimmy that was what he should do. If you watched, and smiled a lot, and were nice, nobody would notice anyway.

"That's only if you're a girl! Besides, I'm not scared. I don't want to watch a bunch of dumb kids jump rope."

Only, that was just part of the truth. What it was was that he never knew what to say around them. What I mean is that a lot of them were hick farm kids. That was what Bo Bo called farmers anyway: hicks. Not that they weren't good people, or anything bad, Bo Bo said, when I had asked him what hicks meant then, if it wasn't bad. Bo Bo said it meant that they didn't pay attention or understand what went on in the real world. He said they thought life was simple, like on a farm.

Jimmy didn't know what to talk about, even to the ones who weren't farm kids. They had more regular parents with regular brothers and sisters. They had dads that went to work at regular jobs and stayed home at night. They did regular things like, they went to Sunday school, church suppers, and took family vacations. They didn't have uncles like Bo Bo that got put in jail. Most of them had parents that probably didn't drink, or swear, or anything. That was why Jimmy didn't want to be around them much. He thought that they would probably think we were weird if they ever knew about us. He was always afraid I was going to tell too much, and they might find out. He didn't want me to have any kids over to the house, either.

I had these two girlfriends, Barb and Anne, over a couple of times. On Saturday, their dads dropped them off, and mine took them home. Jimmy about had a fit! He liked them, but he said they were going to start talking about us to all the kids. It was on account of they kept asking all these questions when they were over. They thought it was sort of strange that Jimmy and me, and our moms and dads, all lived together. They wanted to know where our dads worked. Jimmy looked at me like he would kill me if I told. I said they had some kind of business thing together. Barb wanted to know if it was like a store.

"Yeah!" I said, "Sort of."

She said she wondered because her mom asked her what my dad did.

"Bet you she wouldn't get to come over no more if her mom knew what it was," Jimmy said after she left.

"Maybe she would too! Barb and Anne aren't snotty like some kids."

"Yeah, that's what you think. But what if their moms told them not to play with you?"

So, I didn't ask them to come over anymore, but I still didn't think they would be like that. They asked me to come to their houses. They asked Jimmy, but he wouldn't go. I knew he didn't want me to leave him to have to play alone, but he wouldn't say so.

"Go ahead if you want!"

I knew he didn't mean it, so I stayed home most of the time. Once in a while, I did go. He made kids feel weird around him. They would hardly talk. It wasn't like nobody liked him. It was more like they felt dumb around him. He was so smart. Nobody ever knew what he was thinking. It was like kids were always wondering if he thought they were stupid. He was always nice, but quiet. He would sort of stare like he was waiting for other kids to do the talking. He was serious a lot. He didn't clown around or do silly things like most of the other boys did. It was like he was older. He was more like an older brother to kids.

I knew that wasn't the way he was for real. I was always having to explain it to other kids. I never told him I did. I tried to get him to act different. He was always saying how I wanted everybody to like me, be my friend. I was always so nice-nice—a goody-goody. That was what kind of caused the worst fight we ever got into.

The fight was all over what I told Mrs. King that I shouldn't have. It was after I broke my ankle when she was coming to the house on Saturdays to tutor me. I never would have told her anyway, probably, if it hadn't been for me finding out about Uncle Tommy right before she got there. Jimmy said if I had kept my mouth shut, nobody would have known. Mrs. King blabbed to all the other teachers at school, and then one of the kids overheard it.

On this Saturday, right before she got there, Jimmy came upstairs to my room.

"Guess what?"

"What?"

"Uncle Tommy's in a lot of trouble."

"How?" I said, wondering what Jimmy meant.

"I heard Mom talking to Aunt Flo on the phone. He hit these two kids on bicycles and almost killed them. He was at this bar last night, with another attorney, having a business meeting and drinking martinis. He hit 'em driving home. Dad's getting ready to go to New York."

Jimmy looked at me like he was angry and left the room. A minute later, Mrs. King knocked on my bedroom door.

"Caroline, what's wrong?" she said, first thing.

Like a dummy, I started bawling and told her. Before I could say anything more, she went out to get my mom and saw Jimmy in the hall. Jimmy said she started asking a whole bunch of questions. He told her maybe she should leave. Instead, she went downstairs to talk to our moms. Jimmy came back into my room.

"God, what did you tell her for? Now she's going to blab to the whole school!" he yelled.

When Mrs. King left, we went down to the kitchen. Jimmy was mad and blamed me for telling, and he was mad at Uncle Tommy for doing something stupid.

"For God's sake, Jimmy, stop acting like this! He is your uncle! He made a mistake. He's a good man. You know that people aren't perfect," Pauline said.

"So, big deal, nobody's going to care! He shouldn't have been drinking. People are probably going to say all kinds of bad stuff about him."

Jimmy wouldn't talk to me for two days. Until I started bawling and told him I was sorry for telling.

"Ah, it wasn't your fault, but I told you what would happen!" he said.

Jimmy said that was the big reason you shouldn't tell people things. They'd talk and talk. And the mean ones would cause trouble.

"It's how everybody is around here. They're always talking about everybody. And boy, if they find out anything wrong about you, then they can't wait to tell! That's how grownups are. Most kids are just like 'em too," he said.

"Not all kids, though. Barb and Anne aren't like that. Neither are Lester and Robert. A lot of the other kids aren't either!"

"How do you know? How do you know what they're saying when you're not there?" He said.

"I just know. Everybody's not like that," I said.

"Then how come everybody's talking about Mona?" He said.

"That's different!" I said.

"Yeah, well, I'm sick of hearing 'em," Jimmy said.

CHAPTER NINETEEN

Ever since Mona started seeing Ernie again, everyone was having a fit about it. Jimmy said all they did was "Yak. Yak. Yak." He said they ought to shut up about it and leave Mona alone if she wanted to see creepy Ernie, even if he was a jerk. Alice said her mom was doing it for spite because Alice wouldn't invite her relatives to her wedding and because she knew Alice couldn't stand Ernie. We heard them talking in the kitchen.

"She's going to bring him to the wedding. I know she is," Alice said. "He'll probably make a fool out of himself in front of everybody."

"Alice, will you quit worrying," Mom said. "Ernie's no prize, but he's not that bad!"

"Do you see those clothes he wears? He looks like some carnival jerk! And it's not enough he dresses like some street flasher. He's always bragging and talking loud."

"Honey, there's nothing you can do about it. Anyway, the wedding's still a month off. She still could bring Don!" Mom said.

"Fat chance! I'm telling you she's bringing Ernie on purpose. Tally's relatives are going to die!" Alice said.

"Oh, they aren't either. If they are as nice as you say they are, it's not going to make any difference," Mom said. "Anyway, you're marrying Tally. That's the only thing that's important."

"I know. It's just that I wanted this to be so perfect. Ever since we got engaged, it's been one thing after another. It's like Mom's angry at me all the time. She's always making remarks. I can't say anything, or, right away, she makes it into something."

Mona said it was all on account of the wedding and marrying Tally going to Alice's head.

"I hate to say this," Mona said. "I know Big Jim means well, but I don't think giving Alice this big wedding is good. And I'll tell you something else, and it's not that I don't like Tally, either. It's just that Alice might have picked somebody a little more in her own league."

"Mona, I don't believe I'm hearing this! You were the one that couldn't wait to get them together in the first place!" Mom said.

"Well, maybe I might have made a mistake!"

"You can't be serious! Lord, Mona, what in God's name are you thinking? Even if Alice is acting a little uppity, and I'm going to tell you the truth, I don't think she is, but even if she were, this is ridiculous! You couldn't ask for anyone nicer than Tally."

"I didn't say that! But all of this Catholic business, having to change her religion and all. It's like she wasn't good enough for him and his kind. Then right away, it's the McMillans do this, and the McMillans do that. All hotsie totsie. She had to go to these fancy stores and put her name on the "brides register" for this crystal and silver crap. And another thing, this shit about at first wanting a wedding gown being white. All virginal. I don't give a shit if that first marriage of hers was annulled. I told her so, too! You don't think she didn't sleep with that boy! Bullshit! She's trying to be something she's not!"

"Mona, calm down," Pauline said.

"Well, I don't give a shit. I'm tired of this crap," Mona said. "Let me tell you something; you think if Tally's people knew all about her, knew she'd been married before, knew she had a bunch of hillbillies for relatives, you'd think they'd want her in the family? Bullshit! They'd be on Tally like shit on a stick to dump her like a hot potato! And you know, eventually, they will find out!"

Pauline had to put her arms around Mona. Mona started crying so hard. I heard her and peeked into the kitchen. Once we got back in Jimmy's room, Jimmy said that if Tally's relatives found out, they would probably hate Alice.

"They will not!"

"Well, maybe not hate, but they'd probably not like her," Jimmy said.

When I asked her, Mom said that wasn't so. She said that Alice was a sweet girl, and Tally's folks would like her for herself in time, but Jimmy said differently.

"Oh yeah, blood's thicker than water."

"You're saying that because that's what your dad said once, about Bo Bo's brother being a criminal, and Bo Bo standing up for him, even when he knew it was wrong!" I said.

"So? It's *true.*"

I didn't see how grownups could be like that. How could anybody not like Alice? She was great. Tally loved her. I didn't think it was true. Tally was always talking about his aunts and uncles and cousins, and they sounded terrific.

He had this aunt, Aunt Nadine, and she could speak two languages. She studied at a university in Europe where she lived and where her dad was a professor before she got married to Tally's Uncle William.

Tally had another uncle, and his name was Uncle Michael, which was only one of his names. His whole name was long, and he lived in Scotland, in what Tally said was a fine manor house.

"I was hoping it was a castle," I said when Tally told Jimmy and me and our moms all about it. He wanted to take Alice there to meet his uncle.

Tally laughed. "Some manors are like castles. Caroline, a manor house is what they call them. Why do you like castles?"

"'Cause they're so romantic. I wish I could have been born there like a damsel."

"Like a damsel, Margie, where did you get this one—a *damsel?*" Tally asked my mom.

Jimmy thought I was nutty. He didn't used to, though, when we used to play pretend games, back when we used to be like the Greeks. Now that we were older, we didn't play kid games anymore. Jimmy got funny about anything that was joking around.

Even Missy Greenberg couldn't clown around or kiss Jimmy like she used to, or else he would turn all red. So she stopped. The last time she felt bad afterward, on account of she got him embarrassed.

Missy Greenberg had been out shopping and stopped over after supper to show us this new hat she bought. It was a pretty pink hat, made out of straw, with flowers and a ribbon around the band. This was in the summer when we were all out in the yard. Our yard was sort of a meeting place, like Pauline and Big Jim's Kitchen. When it got warm enough, people met there after dinner to talk. Whoever dropped over would come sit to be together.

That night, Tally and Alice were there, and Penny, Jake, and everybody. Missy Greenberg was parading around modeling the hat. Just being silly. She was trying it on Alice and me, then she put it on Jimmy and tried to spin him around so everyone could see. I thought he was going to die right there! He started blushing. Missy Greenberg felt terrible. She took it off him right away and said she was sorry. Pauline sort of tried to tease him out of it.

"Jimmy! C'mon," she said.

Jimmy said he was going upstairs.

"Where are you going?" Pauline asked.

"Just upstairs," he said.

"Why?" I wanted to know.

"Let him alone," Missy Greenberg said, trying to put her arm around me so I wouldn't pay Jimmy any more attention.

"God, how come he has to be like that!" I said.

"Well, honey, he's getting older, and he's a boy, that's all," Missy Greenberg said.

I knew she meant Jimmy was starting to act grownup. When we were small, Jimmy was the one who always said he was never going to be like grownups. I didn't think there was any sense to say anything. He would only get mad at me and say he didn't want to talk about it. When Jimmy didn't want to talk about something, he could sure clam up.

Jimmy's dad was the same. So was my dad. They didn't like looking dumb or being wrong. My mom said men were that way. I wished Jimmy wouldn't wind up being like them. Mom said men didn't like admitting to being wrong about things, but sometimes they were and wouldn't discuss it. If you were a girl, you should learn that about boys and men. Mom said it was because men looked bigger and stronger than women, so they thought they had to act that way, even if they weren't. Women were just as strong about some things, even stronger. So I thought it was dumb.

Mom and Pauline got in an argument with Big Jim and my dad that turned into being over the same thing. Jimmy and I heard it. We snuck into the living room after dinner and listened. While we were eating, they had started to discuss Missy Greenburg, but didn't say much. We wanted to find out what they probably wouldn't say in front of us.

It started because she had bronchitis. We found out right before Thanksgiving after she had another bad cold that wouldn't go away. The doctor put her in the hospital and did all these tests. Mom and Pauline had been up at the hospital. After we left the room, they told our dads more.

"The doctor says she has to stop smoking," Mom said.

"You think she will?" Dad asked.

"She says she will, but I don't know how she's going to do it. She practically eats those things, she's so nervous," Mom said.

"I don't get what she has to be so nervous about," Dad said.

"C'mon, Merle!" Mom said, sounding like he said something pretty dumb.

"Now, Merle," Pauline said, laughing.

"Well, I don't!" Dad said. "She gets herself all worked up over what she brings on herself."

"Oh, Merle, that's bunk! Betty's always been a worrier if that's what you're talking about. She makes too much out of things, but still, she's had a lot to contend with. Ralph isn't exactly easy to live with. He is stubborn as the day is long." Mom said.

"That's true," Big Jim said. "But I think what Merle is talking about is that she could put a stop to some things, instead of letting it make her a wreck like she does."

"Look, you can't tell me Betty couldn't have put her foot down," Dad said. "She tells story after story, making them funny, about Ralph's hardheadedness, and has all of us in stitches! But you can't laugh about something and let it drive you nuts at the same time."

"But that's Betty's way of coping with things. If she didn't have a sense of humor, she'd probably be in the looney bin by now." Mom said.

"You guys think it's easy to sit here talking about what she should have done," Pauline said. "You try putting up with some of the stuff women have to put up with to get along with a man."

"Ralph doesn't do a thing to make it easier on Betty either," Mom said. "I know he loves her, but he is not exactly the helpful sort. He goes off to work every day at the plant and thinks that is enough. He sits in his easy chair at night and smokes his pipe and reads. He wants his breakfast ready, lunch packed, and his dinner on time. And he doesn't want to do much else or participate in any way."

"I don't give a damn what Ralph does or doesn't do," Dad said. "That's not the point! Hell, Betty has got a mind of her own. You two make it sound like poor Betty. Bullshit! It's because she never says anything. Just pisses and moans and makes jokes about it. It's the same way with that over her wanting to go to beauty school. Christ, she bellyached about it for a month how Ralph didn't want her to go. When she finally did go, all we heard was how bad she felt because Ralph was upset over her not being there when he got home or having dinner on the table. My God, she could have told him she was going, and that was that! Or else, dropped it, and reconciled herself to the way Ralph is."

"It's not always easy to reconcile yourself to something," Pauline said.

"Maybe it's not, but it's certainly better than making yourself a wreck," Big Jim said.

"That may be, but I'd like to see somebody live with somebody, day in and day out, who was always on them about one thing or another without it bothering them. You can't tell me you two could do it!" Mom said.

"That's the point," Big Jim said. "We wouldn't put up with it."

"That's the difference between men and women," Dad said. "Men don't put up with the kind of crap some women do."

"Oh, really!" Mom said, half laughing. "Maybe they don't put up with the same things, but I wouldn't sound so high-and-mighty if I were you. How many times have the two of you put up with all kinds of crap from people around here?"

"Yeah, you guys are always making it sound like it's everybody else that's always having problems because they don't do what they should. The two of you don't always do what you should, either. You're not always right. Only, Lord knows you'd die before you'd admit it!" Pauline said.

"And while we're on the subject," Mom said, "the two of you have been pretty closed-mouthed about what you're going to do if Miller becomes the new Chief of Police."

"And I'll put my two cents worth in on that one right now," Pauline said. "I think you're both kidding yourselves if you think Miller's going to agree to the same arrangement as Kramer did. It's like what Johnny Talbert was saying the other night, things change. It's not so much a case that Miller's such a goody-goody either, but everything is changing."

"Yeah," Mom said. "Out here, especially on this side of town, it's growing like crazy. It's not like everybody knows everybody like they used to. Since the war's been over, people are starting to settle down. Kramer used to say the club was a good thing. It kept the natives off the street. We had one big, happy family for all those years. The club was a place to meet after the bars closed."

"It wasn't just the gambling!" Pauline said. "It was an escape from the war. People didn't want to go home alone. It was a way to fill the hours. People came because they wanted to forget the horror. People had family and friends gone. Well, it's not that way anymore. You can see it happening, Jim. We're starting to get drifters and no counts coming in. And I don't like it!"

"And I don't like it, either," Mom said. "And I'll tell you something else. It's affecting the kids! They act too old for their age. They know too much!"

"Yeah, Jim," Pauline said, "Jimmy especially. I think you guys might think about maybe it's time to close the club?"

It got real quiet. So we went back into Jimmy's room to play cards.

CHAPTER TWENTY

I kept thinking about all the stuff we heard at church when we went with Tally and Alice. I wanted to know if Uncle Tommy was still going to heaven because of having too much to drink and hitting the kids. It was bothering me about what happened. One kid might not ever walk again. Uncle Tommy had to lose his license and, maybe, would even have to go to jail. I wondered if you did something you didn't mean to do, would God let you into heaven? I thought God probably would. Uncle Tommy had been good all his life. Jimmy said God wouldn't.

"You can't go to heaven if you do something awful!"

"But it was an accident."

"So what!"

"He didn't mean to hurt the kids!"

"God! It still doesn't matter. He still did it! He was drinking, or he wouldn't have hit 'em."

"I know you're not supposed to hurt people, and it's a sin. But why would you have to go to hell, or that place in between, that purgatory. I'm going to ask Mom what she thinks," I said.

When I came out of Jimmy's room, I saw Dad coming out of Big Jim's study, so I asked him.

"Lord, Caroline, I don't know. That's between Uncle Tommy and his maker. But I would think what he did would carry a pretty stiff penalty. Why don't you go ask your mom what she thinks? She's downstairs in the laundry room."

"Mom, do you think God will let Uncle Tommy go to heaven? Jimmy says Uncle Tommy won't because what he did was too wrong to get into heaven. I asked Dad, and he said it was pretty bad, but to ask you."

"I don't know, honey, but I don't think it's that simple. Jimmy's looking at it from the standpoint that what Uncle Tommy did was what the Bible says are some of the worst sins. But the Bible also talks about judging everything a person does. Now, Uncle Tommy did a lot of good in his life, and God will probably weigh all that, and if the good outweighs the bad, then he would probably let Uncle Tommy into heaven. God believes in the forgiveness of sins. We are to forgive others as God forgives us. But those things aren't for us to know. We just have to hope for the best, honey."

I went back and told Jimmy that it wasn't that simple, that God would weigh everything, and that if the good outweighed the bad, Uncle Tommy might still go to heaven.

"Yeah, if God weighs like Mona does!" Jimmy laughed.

I didn't think it was so funny. Jimmy thought it was a hilarious joke. We had overheard Mona talking to Pauline the day before. She had been trying to defend why she was seeing Ernie again, and she said that the good outweighed the bad.

"I know everybody thinks I'm nuts for seeing him again," Mona said. "Ernie's changed a lot, Pauline. He's settled down. And I still care about him. I can't help it!"

"But Mona, okay, granted, Ernie's got a steady job now, and he works every day, and he's not chasing all over town supposedly, but still, how can you trust him? My Lord, Mona, the man walked out on you when you were pregnant!"

"I know, but it wasn't all his fault, either. I knew he didn't want any kids. He said he didn't want to go raising a bunch of kids the way his ma and pa had, never having anything. But I was tired of waiting. He kept saying maybe when he made it big in racing, but I was getting older. Besides, you know when that would have been. *Never!* So I got that way on purpose. I know it was dumb, but I guess I thought he'd marry me anyway. Once the baby came, it'd be okay. But he knew it wasn't any accident."

"I don't care if it wasn't any accident. There is such a thing as responsibility! It was still no damn excuse for him to walk off and leave you. Especially after you miscarried and almost died!"

"But he didn't plan to leave me for good. He said he did it to teach me a lesson. He said he wanted me to stew in my own juice for a while. Then he was coming back."

"And you believe that?"

"Yes, I do, Pauline. I'm tired of being alone. I want a home of my own. Alice is all but gone now. I don't want to live the rest of my life alone. I've worked and slaved most of my life, and I'm sick of it! After my husband was killed, I had to raise Alice all by myself. I was so young! You don't know what it's like, not being able to get a decent job, working in bars, but mostly doing everything myself. Never having anybody to lean on."

"What about Don Andrews? I mean, Lord, the man is nuts about you, Mona! Listen to me. I understand what you're saying. I don't blame you a bit for feeling like you do, but what I can't figure is why it has to be Ernie? I mean, you couldn't ask for a better man than Don. He treats you like gold, for God's sake! The man has a good job. You could have all the things you've always wanted, a nice home, and you could travel. Not have to worry about bills for once in your life. You two could build a real life together. Even if Ernie has changed, he can't possibly give you the security Don can."

"That's not the only thing important, you know. Ernie may have faults in some areas, but he is very good in one department, if you know what I mean. There the good outweighs the bad by a long shot! And I'm not exactly over the hill yet."

"Oh. c'mon, you might not be over the hill, but you're certainly not a teenager either, Mona! By now, you should know that that kind of physical attraction won't last forever."

"Oh, I know, but it's a lot of other things too that I just can't explain. Don's a really terrific person, and he treats me great, all right. That I can't deny, but he's not perfect either, Pauline."

"So, nobody's perfect."

"I know that. It's with Don; it's harder to explain. He doesn't drink or run around, and he has a good job, and he's good to me and polite, and all that. I don't know. Maybe it's just me, but he is always wanting me right there next to him and always expects me to do everything with him. Like he wants me to hold his hand twenty-four hours a day. Like he's a little boy, still a kid."

"Mona, you can't have everything! Look, I can't tell you what to do, but Mona, please don't go running off with Ernie and getting rid of Don until you think this through," Pauline said.

Mom said Mona didn't know what she wanted most was her big problem. Only, that wasn't what Mom said about Jake when she wanted to leave Penny. Jimmy and I overheard all about that, too. It turned into a mess.

Mom said that Jake knew damn well what she wanted. Mom said Penny knew what Jake wanted all right. Only, Penny didn't want to accept it. Mom said Penny's biggest problem was that she was afraid of being alone, not that she was so madly in love with Jake.

Jake was the first person that was extra nice and understanding to Penny after her fiancé walked out on her. He walked out on her after she had to have an operation called a hysterectomy. It took out all her female parts, so she could never have any kids.

Jake used to come into the bank where Penny worked. That was how Penny knew her. That was when Penny was still a teller, the person that hands out all the money when you come in to get checks cashed. When Penny was in the hospital, Jake sent her flowers and came up to visit her. She came up the night Penny's fiancé told her he couldn't marry her. Penny said they didn't know when she went in that they were going to take out all the parts. She said her fiancé was acting funny after the operation and she knew something was wrong. When she asked him if he still loved her, even if she couldn't have kids, he started bawling and said he couldn't help it, but he couldn't marry her anymore. He ran out of the room. A little later, Jake came up.

Jake told her a lot of men were like that. You couldn't trust them. When you needed them the most, was when they walked out on you.

Penny said she didn't have many friends, or anything, on account of her moving to our town not long before with her mom, so her mom could be near her aunt after her dad died of a heart attack. Plus, she said she didn't make friends easily, either.

When she had her female parts removed, she didn't have anybody to turn to outside of the people at work. They were nice, but not really friends.

"When Jake came along, I needed somebody, and she was just there. It wasn't anything I thought out. I'd never done anything like that before. I've never had a lot of boyfriends, but it wasn't like I wasn't attracted to boys. I suppose it was that I was so shy," Penny said.

"How did you wind up moving in with her?" Mom asked.

"One thing just led to another. It's funny, but I don't even think I admitted to myself what we were involved in. I know that sounds stupid, but Jake was the first person besides Jed, my fiancé, that ever treated me like a real person. All my life, it's always been me taking care of everybody else."

"What do you mean?" Mom asked.

"My parents were so much older when they had me that it was like they were my grandparents. I am an only child and a change of life baby. By the time I was a teenager, my dad was old, retired, and in a bad way from heart trouble, and my mom was having problems getting around from arthritis. So I stayed home a lot to take care of them. I was so painfully shy, but even if I hadn't been, I wouldn't have had much time to date. My parents were good people. They loved me, but I didn't think they ever wanted me."

"Oh, honey," Mom said.

"Oh, I can't blame them either! After all those childless years, to suddenly have a child dumped in your lap. Even their friends who had children had grown ones and grandkids by then. I think my mom was plain embarrassed."

"How old was she?"

"She turned fifty the year after I was born."

"Lord!"

"Yeah, can you imagine? Having your first one at that age! Especially in a little town of two thousand people where everybody practically knew everybody, and my dad being a high school English teacher in the only high school in town. Boy, the jokes that must have flown around! My father was so proper, anyways. He probably nearly died. He'd probably roll over in his grave if he knew about Jake and me."

"Does your mom know?"

"No, she just thinks that Jake is a friend. I couldn't do that to her. I never even told her about why Jed left me."

"My Lord, why?"

"Because I couldn't do that to her. My mother's old, Pauline! It's like she's not my mother. I know she is, of course, but I've never felt like I could talk to her like a mother. It's like she doesn't want to know anything that isn't good. She wants me to go along, being this uncomplicated daughter. So did my dad. My father was a scholarly man, and he taught me the love I have for books, but that's all he was ever interested in. It was fine, as long as I went to school and got good grades. He'd sit up all night and discuss literature, or art, with me. But if I had any kind of problem, that was different. He didn't want to hear it. So I never had anybody I could talk to like I can talk to Jake."

"So, what are you going to do now?" Mom asked.

"I don't know. I keep hoping Jake will change her mind."

"I don't think she's going to do that," Pauline said.

"Yeah, I know. She hasn't been coming home at night. And I know she's been seeing someone else. At first, I kept trying to ignore it, hoping it'd blow over."

"Why don't you move back with your mom and aunt?" Mom suggested.

"Oh, I don't want to do that. My aunt's a sweet person, but she's used to being alone. With my mom, it is fine, but when I was there, it got to be a strain. Jake thinks I ought to go to college like my dad wanted before he died. He set aside a trust fund for me. That's what I was sort of planning to do when I met Jed, right after we moved here. When he asked me to marry him, I stayed with the job at the bank."

"I think it's a good idea. You're a smart girl, and you've got your whole life ahead of you." Mom said. "There's no reason you can't go out there and make something of yourself. Not everyone has the opportunity to go to college."

"I feel so foolish. It will soon be going on four years now since I've been out of high school. Everybody's going to be so much younger than me."

"Oh, Penny, not everybody's going to be younger than you," Mom said. "Lord, you make it sound like three or four years is ancient."

"I know, but I'm not going to know anybody. Jake said she'd help me find an apartment by the university, but the university is clear across town. I don't know what I'm going to do."

CHAPTER TWENTY-ONE

I was afraid I wasn't going to get to be in Alice's wedding because of my broken ankle. Only, on the bottom of my cast, the doctor finally put a metal disk so I could walk on it. I had a long, red velvet dress. Mom made a red velvet sock to fit over my foot and the cast. Alice said not to worry, that no one would notice. We had to walk slowly in the procession anyway, so it wasn't so hard not to limp.

Tally's friend, Jeff, was his best man, and Pauline was the matron of honor. At first, Pauline said she was too old and didn't want to do it.

"Oh, I'd feel foolish!"

"Please, Pauline. I don't want anyone else," Alice kept begging.

So Pauline couldn't say no. She was matron of honor, and three of Tally's cousins were bridesmaids. Jimmy wore a black tuxedo. Alice wanted him to wear a white suit, but he wouldn't. Jimmy said if he was going to be in the wedding, he wanted to look like the rest of the men. All the women wore red velvet long dresses. The women carried gardenias tied with red and green velvet ribbon. I got to carry a little basket of white and peach-colored roses like the roses Alice carried, only hers were surrounded with lace and long ribbons trailing down. She was so beautiful. She looked like a fairy princess. She wore a satin gown with a big train. Big Jim gave her away.

Pauline said that Big Jim was so choked up she thought he was going to cry when the priest asked, "Who gives this woman in holy matrimony?" Big Jim stepped up next to Tally and handed Alice by the arm to him. When he did, Big Jim saw tears in Tally's eyes, and his eyes got teary too.

Jimmy said I was beautiful. He kissed me on the cheek. He did it downstairs, where it was almost dark. It was while we were alone, before anyone came out in the hall, as the people were being seated upstairs in the church.

"I wish I didn't have to wear this dumb cast," I said, while we waited. "Everybody is going to know."

"Nobody will, they'll all be looking at how pretty you look," Jimmy said, not looking at me.

"You really think so?" I asked.

"Yeah, I'm going to go upstairs and watch the people come in. You better stay down here till it's time."

When it came time to go down the aisle, Jimmy was as scared as I was, but he didn't look like it. He looked real handsome. When I told him he looked handsome, he started to blush, and like always, whenever he got embarrassed, he stared at the floor. He knew I knew why he did it. So when he looked up, I looked down at the floor. We both started to laugh like it was a joke.

"What if I trip?" I said, getting scared.

"You're not gonna trip!" Jimmy said.

"But what if I do?"

"You're not gonna, watch me if you think you're gonna."

I only had to look at him once. It was right at the middle

when I thought we were never going to make it to the altar. It was taking so long.

The altar was all lit with candles because it was a candle-light wedding close to Christmas Eve, my birthday. I told Jimmy that was when I wanted us to have our wedding too. It made it extra, extra special. The priest said it was a magical time. He was talking about it being close to Baby Jesus' birthday. Mom said that maybe that was why everything went so perfect with the wedding.

One of the best things that happened was that Mona brought Don Andrews, instead of Ernie. At the reception, Don said he had an announcement. He stood up and told everybody that he and Mona were getting married. Everybody made a toast. Mom said it was too good to be true. Pauline said it was the happiest wedding she had ever seen.

I loved all the romantic stuff the best: the candles, and everybody crying, and the way Tally kept looking at Alice after the wedding, like she was so princess beautiful, and all during the reception the way they kept staring at each other like it was a fairytale. Jimmy said it was so stupid. Not like he meant it, more like it was embarrassing because I wouldn't shut up about it. When the band started playing, they turned the lights out so nothing was on but the candles, so Alice and Tally could dance the first dance. As we watched, Jimmy slipped his fingers through mine in the folds of my dress.

The band played this beautiful waltz about being wed. Tally and Alice looked so regal. They kept looking into each other's eyes as they danced around the room. It was so quiet, with only the sound of the music and the swishes of all the ladies' velvet and taffeta dresses.

When it was over, they turned up the lights, and everybody danced. I wanted Jimmy to dance with me. He said maybe. Only, I knew he probably wouldn't do it because he'd be too shy. Later on, after he drank some champagne that our moms let us have because it was a special night, he did. Only, this stupid woman had to go and say, "Oh, isn't that cute!" Everybody started saying things about how cute we were.

Jimmy stopped dancing and wouldn't dance anymore.

When I went out to find the restroom, I heard Tally and Alice talking. Everybody was inside dancing, and Tally and Alice were standing by these big doors watching outside, with their arms around one another.

"It's almost too good to be true, snow right before Christmas at our wedding. How many people do you think are this lucky?" Alice said.

"Not many, but then maybe we're fated for good things," Tally said, laughing.

"I'm serious, don't joke!" Alice said.

"I'm not, silly. Why shouldn't we be fated? Aren't we as good as anybody?"

"Yes, of course, we are. But it sounds, I don't know, pompous or something."

"Alice, darling, nothing bad is going to happen to us."

"Everything is so wonderful! I'm afraid sometimes. I've never been this happy in my life, Tally. Everything I've ever wanted is coming true."

"Honey, why shouldn't it?"

"Because it hasn't always been that way!"

"I know, honey, but the past is behind you. From now on, you are Mrs. Tally McMillian."

"Oh, that sounds wonderful. Mrs. Tally McMillian," Alice said.

"Turn around here. Let me look into those beautiful, beautiful, beautiful eyes," Tally said. "Alice, listen to me. I want you to always remember this, our life together might not always be as perfect as it's been up to now, honey, but your past is over.

It's you and me, and we've got a new life together. We're going to raise a family, a big family, Alice, and we're going to fill it with love, and we're going to have a home, a real home, and we're going to fill it with kids, and someday when we're old and gray, we're going to fill it with grandkids. We're going to go on picnics, and to the beach, and do all the things we always dreamed we'd do together."

"Oh, Tally, I love you!"

"I love you too. I love you! I love you, Alice!"

Only, that's not the way it was. My mom said, all those plans of the *happy ever after* almost didn't happen.

Tally got shot in the summer when Alice was pregnant. Rotten Ben Beacon, who Jimmy always said, would kill somebody—shot him at the club. He hurt him real bad. And killed another guy.

CHAPTER TWENTY-TWO

"Tommy, seven times six?"

"Forty-two."

"Jean, four times nine?"

"Thirty-six."

"Robert, five times five?"

"Ah—"

"Michael? Five times five?"

"Twenty-five."

That is how Miss Bissell made us do our multiplication tables in fourth grade. That is how Miss Bissell made us do everything—out loud and fast. In front of everybody, standing up. She was the worst teacher in the school, and I got her. She had almost black hair she colored that way, and it looked weird. In some places, it would be dark, and in others, it would be burned looking. You could always tell when she did it. There would be brown marks on her neck that would be red from rubbing like she tried to get the color off but couldn't. When she was bending over at another kid's desk in front of you, you could see them. I used to think they looked like her real self—red and angry.

She wore black-rimmed glasses that had rhinestones on the tops. Only, they weren't glamorous. The glass was so thick they made her eyes look bugged out. It made me hate rhinestones. She wore red lipstick that would get into the wrinkles around her mouth and on her teeth. She never smiled. The kids called her prune face behind her back. Her lips were always all puckered up in class like she was mad.

She walked all the time when she was talking or making us answer questions. She walked up and down the aisles and around the room outside the desks. She carried a ruler.

The worst was when you would hear her coming up behind you, or when she would call your name. If you didn't know the answer fast enough, she would go on to somebody else. Sometimes she wouldn't—if maybe she was feeling mean.

"Caroline, eight times nine?"

"Caroline! Eight times nine?"

"Who knows the answer? Richard?"

"Seventy-two."

"Richard, turn around and tell Caroline!"

"Seventy-two."

"Caroline, how come you don't know the answer? Don't stand there staring! Haven't you been studying?"

"I guess."

"You guess what? That you have been studying or that you haven't been studying?"

"I've been sort of."

"Been sort of?"

"I've been studying some."

"You've been studying some. Well, you haven't been studying enough, have you?"

"No."

"Speak up!"

"No."

"You had better start studying enough! That goes for the rest of you also. Anybody in here that gets called, and doesn't have the right answer, after a time or two, is going to be spending every recess filling the blackboard. Caroline, you can start right now! Eight times nine in columns. Side and front blackboards both. And print small!"

There wasn't any chalk when I got up there. I kept praying and praying that the recess bell would ring before Miss Bissell noticed I wasn't writing. I just kept thinking, please, God, please, make it ring. First off, I was so scared I couldn't remember how much eight times nine was. All these numbers kept flying in my head. I was shaking so hard I couldn't stay still to think it up.

"Jeff, nine times seven?"

"Sixty—two, no wait, sixty-three? No, sixty-two?"

"Well, which is it?"

"Ah, sixty-three, sixty-three."

"Bill, four times—Caroline, why aren't you writing?"

"There isn't any chalk."

"There is some up in the top drawer of my desk. Next time ask!"

"Judy, four times six?"

"Twenty-four."

"Ralph, five times seven?"

"Ah, ah—"

"Cindy?"

"Thirty-five."

"Ralph, seven times eight—just a minute. Caroline, what are you doing? Why aren't you writing?"

"Cuz, I forgot how much it was."

"What did you forget?"

159

"The answer."

"The answer to what? What are the numbers?"

"Eight times nine."

"Richard, would you please stand up and tell Caroline again what the answer is! Maybe this time, she'll remember it!"

"Seventy-two."

Then the bell rang.

"Everybody just stay right in your seats! Stay right in your seats! You're not in school for recess. I didn't dismiss anyone, yet. Most of what we have been doing is no more than review. You had most of it in the third grade, and there's no excuse for not knowing it. I can tell you when you get out of this class you're going to know it! You're going to know everything you should know in the fourth grade or else I'm not going to pass you. So if you're having problems with something, you'd better come and talk to me. I'll arrange to work with you at lunch or recess. And another thing, when that bell rings, I expect you to file out of here calmly, not race like you've been doing. All right, you can go now."

I hated her! She was the only teacher I ever hated. I kept hoping if I was nice to her, she would like me, but she got meaner. I even went to her at recess for help. At first, she was pretty nice, saying that if you didn't know something, you should always ask. She said how most kids wouldn't ask for help, like she was glad I did. I thought it was going to get better, but then she told me I wasn't trying hard enough.

"You can't tell me you're not smart enough to learn this. You don't want to. You're always sitting over in that corner daydreaming. You better snap out of it!"

That was how she was. She would watch you, waiting to catch you doing something wrong, so she could get you for it, and make you look stupid in front of the whole class.

The worst thing happened right before the school year was

over. She found this red notebook of mine. I forgot and left it in my desk. In it were these stories I wrote. She read them. I didn't even know it was missing until she took it out of her desk drawer at lunch recess. She told me to stay after, in the room, because she wanted to talk to me about something. When all the other kids left, she told me to come up and sit at the desk right in front of hers.

"The reason I told you to stay is that I found something in your desk that I want to talk to you about."

The minute she took out the notebook and held it up, I wished I could just die!

"Seems this is the reason you're barely passing some subjects. Instead of paying attention in class, you're dreaming up stories. Tell me, Caroline, where do you get your ideas? This one, for instance, titled *Miss Prune Lips*," she said, holding up the page for me to see, then handing it to me.

"Go ahead and read it out loud, start right here, no, on second thought—start here. Go ahead!"

"So the teacher was always yelling—"

"Louder, Caroline! I can barely hear you. Start over!"

"So the teacher was always yelling at the little girl and making her stay at recess. The little girl started being extra nice and smiling at the teacher. The little girl cleaned the teacher's erasers and blackboards. One day, the little girl wrote the teacher a poem and put it into a little book tied with a blue ribbon. She left it on the teacher's desk. The poem told about how the little girl didn't think the teacher was a mean teacher like she acted. It told how she—"

"You can stop right there! Who's the teacher?"

"You are."

"Speak up!"

"You are."

"Of course, and the little girl is you. It's a lovely story, isn't

CAROLINE SHANNON DAVENPORT

it? The mean, wicked teacher needs someone to love her and is won over by the sweet little girl. The little girl sees the teacher is a kind-hearted lady underneath. Well, I'll give you this much, you've got a good imagination, and you're certainly descriptive enough! I especially like the part about the lipstick and the rhinestone glasses! That's all right—no need to look down. I know what I look like. Although I have to admit, I didn't think it was quite so bad. And I don't think I'm quite the cruel witch you've portrayed. Although, I know I'm not the teacher most children would prefer. Do you know why?"

"No."

"Oh, I think you do! I think you want to fool yourself. The reason is that I make my students work. I don't care whether you children like me or not. I'm here to teach you and to make you learn. Some foolish children like you don't understand the importance of learning. But you will later if you don't listen to me. First, I want to ask you some questions. How long have you been writing stories like this?"

"Since first grade."

"Why do you write them?"

"Because I like to."

"Is that the only reason?"

"It's because I'm going to be a writer when I grow up."

"Oh, so that's it! So you think because you write stories you're going to be a writer, do you? You've got a lot to learn yet, Caroline. To start with, how to spell and punctuate. It takes years of training to be a good writer. Even then, that doesn't guarantee that you'll be a success. This may come as a surprise to you, but when I was your age, I wanted to be an actress. I was just as sure as you are right now that it would work out. Only it didn't."

"How come?"

"Oh, I guess I wasn't as good as I thought I was. I studied

drama in college. After I finished school, I performed at a local playhouse for a while. I thought I was on top of the world. Of course, I didn't look like I look now. I was young and pretty. I had lots of beaus. But I wasn't interested in anything but being an actress. When I finally had enough money saved up, I went to New York. But I didn't realize how many other young and pretty girls, just like me, there would be. So finally, when I couldn't pay my bills on the few small parts I got playing Off-Broadway, I came home.

"Don't look so sad! I wasn't the only one. There were a lot of other girls that had their dreams dashed. But I was luckier than most. Years before, someone had talked to me the way I'm talking to you now. At the time, I was a little bit older than you, but the point is, they made me realize that being an actress wasn't the only thing in the world. I still needed to study other things. In college, I took courses, so I could be a teacher."

"But I don't want to be anything else but a writer!"

"Well, I didn't want to be anything else but be an actress, either. Unfortunately, life doesn't always turn out the way we want it. It's not like one of your stories that you write, so everything will come out the way you wish it. You can't change everything around in real life. You're playing a game of pretend with that notebook filled with fantasy stories. The story about the two children and the good man that hit them was about your uncle, wasn't it?"

"Yes."

"And we both know that the story you wrote isn't the truth. I know you think I'm terribly cruel now, but maybe if you listen to me, you won't someday. You've got to stop this, not paying attention in class and not studying. You've already flunked one grade. You don't want to flunk another one, do you?"

"No."

"You are a very smart girl, but you're stubborn, and if you

are not careful, that stubbornness is going to get you in a lot of trouble. You think you can just smile that sweet smile of yours and get away with doing what you want. Maybe you can fool some teachers, but you can't get through school like that. I'm going to keep this notebook of yours until the last day. Then you can have it back. In the meantime, I don't want to find another one in your desk, and when I look in your direction, I don't want to see that dreamy look on your face anymore. Is that understood?"

"Yes."

"Once you leave this class, I can't do anything about how you get along. But I'm telling you for your own good, snap out of this, or you're headed for real problems."

CHAPTER TWENTY-THREE

The first week school was out for the summer, my mom, dad, and I moved. Dad bought a restaurant, not far from where we lived. It had a big apartment on the top floor. My mom and dad were going to run the restaurant. They said it was easier if we lived right above it. Big Jim and Dad had to close the club on account of a new police chief who wouldn't take any money to let them stay open. They wanted to close it anyway, after what Beacon did. My dad said it could never be the same.

Jimmy and me only lived a few blocks away from each other. I liked living in the same house better, even though we got to see each other just as much. We spent the whole summer together over at Jake and Beth's new house. Beth was the woman Jake started seeing after Penny moved out. Penny went to live in an apartment by the university so she could go to school. Pauline and Mom, everybody really, thought she made a good decision. Jake helped her move. The good part was they were still friends. Penny still came to visit us at Pauline and Big Jim's.

Right behind the restaurant that my dad bought, and where we lived, a whole bunch of these little houses that all looked sort of alike were built. Jake bought one, and Beth moved in with her.

After Jake bought the house, she had some construction guys she knew put this huge pool in her backyard. She took a week of her vacation to help. Jimmy and me went over and watched them build it. When it was done, we all went swimming almost every day. Jake and Beth worked the afternoon shift at the factory where they made Jeeps. They didn't have to go into work until later.

That was the summer Jimmy and me learned how to swim. Jake was good at going off the diving board. I didn't like it, because if you didn't do it right, you could do a belly smacker. I was always doing belly smackers. Jimmy did pretty good dives. I didn't think he would because he hated heights. He kept telling me to jump without thinking. Not to look down. Only, I'd start thinking about how bad it was going to feel if I hit wrong. Then, I'd mess up.

One thing that was fun was that we would float around on inner tubes. We would float around and watch the clouds make different formations. Once, when Jimmy and me were alone— Jake was still sleeping, and Beth was reading a novel—I told Jimmy I wished we could stay right there forever. It was so peaceful and perfect.

"God, don't you wish we could stay like this forever and ever. Stay floating around, feeling the sun, and watching the clouds?"

"Yeah, but we can't," he said.

"But we could pretend like we could."

"Uh-huh."

"Don't you think we could?" I said.

"I said, yeah!" he said.

"I mean, really pretend."

"You can't really pretend," he said.

"Yes, you can!"

"Okay, how?" he asked.

"Well, when you're pretending, like when you are imagining something, it's real at the time. I mean, it doesn't feel like pretending, so it's real!" I said.

"It is not!"

"How come you used to do it? You used to think it was real when we'd pretend something," I said.

"Yeah, when you're a kid. But that's because you're playing."

"So, why can't you pretend to be playing now?" I asked.

"How am I supposed to pretend to be playing when I know I'm playing?"

"C'mon, you could try. You used to do it! Just stare at the clouds, okay? Just keep staring. Keep staring. Okay, keep feeling how nice it is. Don't think about anything else. Think about only now, and keep watching the clouds, and keep staring," I said.

"I can't do it," he said.

At the start of the school year, in the fifth grade, we both got the same teacher. We got Mr. Stanhope. He was new at our school and the first man teacher in the whole school. I liked him right off. He had a flat top, and wore glasses, and was extra nice. He told me his wife's name was Caroline, like mine, and that she even looked a little like me. He said she wore her hair real short and had tiny features like I did.

He told us about himself on the first day. He said he had been teaching for six years at a school in Indiana, near where he was raised. He said that they moved to be closer to his wife's parents. He said he met his wife in Indiana while they were in college, and his wife was going to have a baby soon.

"Well, what do you think?" I asked Jimmy.

"About Mr. Stanhope?"

"Don't you think he's extra nice? Don't you think he's about the best teacher here?" I asked.

"Yeah, I guess. But God, it's only the first day!" he said.

"So what! You can tell on the first day."

"Not always. Sometimes teachers just start out acting nice." Jimmy said.

Mr. Stanhope never changed. He stayed nice. He was like Mr. Hess, the principal. Only, he was religious. He taught Sunday school at the Baptist Church. He didn't talk a lot about it in class. He didn't say religious stuff to everyone like Ben Beacon did after he "got religion," as dad called it. I found out Mr. Stanhope was religious when I asked him to help me with my math and English. Sometimes after he got finished helping, especially when it was recess and we were alone in the room, we talked about all kinds of things.

"Do you go to church?" he asked me one day.

"No. I did once. I went a few times to a Catholic church with these friends of my parents."

"Do your parents go?" He asked.

"No, my mom thinks that you don't need church to be religious. My mom says that the important thing is that you believe in God and are a good person. That you don't tell lies and you obey the Ten Commandments. My dad thinks a lot of people just go to church to show off. He says they go to try to convince themselves, or other people, that they are good people."

"Some people might do that, but not everyone."

When he said that, I was thinking of what my dad talked about that Jimmy and me overheard about people that came into the club. Dad said how they would gamble all night, knowing it was against their religion, but then get up the next morning and go to church. He said how the churches even knew gambling in our club was going on, how they were hypocrites. Churches winked and looked the other way. He said everybody knew, but they wouldn't allow it to be legal and that no politician could ever get elected if they tried to make it legal. I didn't tell Mr. Stanhope about that part Dad said. I said I didn't think it was everyone, either.

"Most people go because they sincerely want to worship the Lord, and the church is the Lord's home here on earth. So, it's natural that people would want to go to church," Mr. Stanhope said.

"But what if you don't go to church? My mom always says you can pray to God any place. He'll hear you."

"Your mom's right. God hears all our prayers whenever we pray. He's there listening. We are all God's children, and he loves all his children. In fact, he loves us so much, he sent his only son to die on the cross, so we might be forgiven our sins. All God asks is that we accept his son, Jesus, into our hearts, and we'll be saved for all eternity."

I didn't say anything to Jimmy about Mr. Stanhope being religious. After what happened with Ben Beacon, Jimmy would probably have thought Mr. Stanhope was sort of crazy, too, if he knew about how Mr. Stanhope talked about God and Jesus. When we were talking, just the two of us, Mr. Stanhope was always using words like, *The Lord*. He would say, *The Lord* said this, or *The Lord* said that. Sort of the way Beacon had always gone on about *The Lord*.

Once, when Mr. Stanhope said, *The Lord* in class, when we were discussing something, Jimmy looked at him suspiciously, like he was wondering if Mr. Stanhope was maybe another weirdo.

After Beacon went nuts and shot up the club, Jimmy's dad said Beacon used religion. Before he shot up the place, Beacon was always going on about The Lord forgiving your sins. Dad said in Beacon's crazy mind, he probably thought that would get him off the hook for killing someone. He was just looking for a way out for what he wanted to do—kill people. Dad said that's what most people wanted to do: have an excuse for the worst things they did.

I didn't think Mr. Stanhope was like that at all. I felt he was sincere, even if sometimes he sounded almost like Beacon. We didn't only talk about religion. We talked about all sorts of things. The thing that I liked best about Mr. Stanhope was that he never got mad. He never yelled in class. About the only thing he would do was rap the desk with a book if kids were messing around, not listening. Nobody disobeyed him or made jokes about him because he was so nice. If you didn't know something, he would tell you the answer, then explain it. He never made anybody feel like a dumbbell. He didn't have a favorite, either. No teacher's pets! I mean, I knew he liked me a lot because we talked, but he didn't treat me different from the other kids.

It's funny, I thought at the beginning that he wasn't going to like me once he found out that I was bad in math and English, but he never said anything about it. He never acted like it was awful. He believed that if you worked on something, you would get better at it. He never made a big deal out of stuff you were bad at, just out of stuff you are good at. He was patient about helping you with things. I started to like school for once. Jimmy thought the reason was that I liked Mr. Stanhope.

"It is not! He makes everything so easy is why."

"Yeah, you got a crush on him!" Jimmy laughed.

One night after school, Jimmy called on the phone.

"Guess what?"

"I already know. Bo Bo's home. Mom told me."

"Yeah, when you comin' over?"

"Want me to come over now?"

"Yeah."

Bo Bo got out of prison that morning. He was coming over to Jimmy's for dinner. Mom and Dad, and Pauline and Big Jim, and Jimmy and me were all going to be there. Pauline had been cooking Italian-style spaghetti. Bo Bo's favorite. Mom even made strawberry shortcake though fresh strawberries were out of season. She made them from some she had frozen. They weren't like fresh ones, but Mom's strawberry shortcake was Bo Bo's favorite.

When he was in prison, Pauline had only seen Bo Bo once, when she went with Big Jim. Dad and Big Jim had seen him the most. Mom and Jimmy and me hadn't seen him at all. Mom and Pauline had made him a lot of stuff and sent it with our dads. Jimmy and me wrote him a letter a couple of times. It seemed strange that he was going to be home. It seemed to me like he had been gone a long, long time.

"It seems like he's been gone forever!"

"Yeah," Jimmy said.

While we were waiting for him to come, everybody seemed nervous, like they wished he would hurry up, so seeing him again for the first time after jail would be over with fast. It was like everybody wanted things back to normal, not upsetting. I kept trying to think what I should say to him, but I couldn't think of anything. Pauline kept pushing back the curtains to look out the window.

"Pot never boils while you watch it," Mom said.

Big Jim made martinis. Our dads never drank much. My dad said drinking caused too many problems for people, but they said this was a special occasion, and because Bo Bo liked them. Only then they started talking about business and acting like seeing Bo Bo was no big deal. Jimmy was acting the same way.

"C'mon, let's play checkers," Jimmy said.

"Are you nuts!" I said. "I don't want to play checkers. I want to wait for Bo Bo."

"You can still wait for Bo Bo and play checkers!"

"I can't neither. Maybe you can, but I can't!"

When we heard the sound of car crunching the gravel in the driveway and a car door slam, everybody got quiet. Big Jim was staring into his martini. My dad got up to get ice out of the refrigerator. Mom was standing by the sink where she had been washing lettuce for the salad, kind of glancing out the door waiting, with her hand still on the faucet like she was frozen. Pauline was stirring the spaghetti sauce really slow. Jimmy was looking down, kicking the iron leg of the table with his foot. I was watching everybody and listening to Bo Bo coming up the stairs. When the door slammed on the second landing, Pauline looked up from the spaghetti. I could see her bottom lip quivering.

All of a sudden, he was there, standing in the doorway.

"Whatsa kinda welcome is this?" Bo Bo said, sounding Italian and smiling like crazy.

Then, Bo Bo was hugging Pauline and Mom. I was behind them, and Jimmy was behind me, with Dad and Big Jim gathered around. Pauline and Mom and I were all crying, and at the same time, trying not to. Bo Bo was saying silly things, like he was going to need a life jacket soon, in order to make us quit.

"Oh, shut up! Always the smart mouth!" Pauline said, laughing and wiping her eyes.

"Jimmy, boy!" Bo Bo said, shaking Jimmy's hand, and grinning. "My God, look how you two kids have grown. Caroline! Give me a twirl around! Oooooh, thatsa nice!"

At dinner, everybody was talking at once. Bo Bo wanted to know about what everyone was doing, Mona and Missy Greenberg, and everybody. He couldn't quit saying how he couldn't believe how big Jimmy and me had gotten. He only stayed for about an hour after dinner. He had to go see some other friends. He played one game of Chinese checkers with Jimmy and me first, though. After he left, Pauline said she thought Bo Bo looked older.

"Maybe he's grown up," Dad said.

"I would hope so!" Big Jim said. "If he hasn't learned his lesson by now and is ready to play straight and settle down, he's never going to!"

CHAPTER TWENTY-FOUR

Boy, did Bo Bo ever turn out to be ready to settle down. He started bringing this woman named Jo around right after he met her, for everybody to get to know. Not even a whole six weeks later, at Pauline and Big Jim's in the morning for coffee, he said he was getting married in two days. Just like that! He wanted Big Jim and Pauline to stand up for him at the courthouse.

Pauline and Mom rushed around planning and calling everybody all afternoon to put a reception party together for afterward. But Pauline nearly killed him for it happening so fast and not giving them more time to plan.

"Pauline, don't start!" Bo Bo said. "Don't make this into a deal. That's why Jo and I are doing it this way."

"Aw, c'mon, you got to have something!"

"Keep it small, okay? Just a few people, no more, okay?"

"Okay, okay, just a few people!"

The reason why Bo Bo said they didn't want to make a deal out of it was they had been married before, to other people. Pauline said it was when they were young, but she told my mom that wasn't the only reason. Mainly, it was because Jo's dad was a big honcho banker in town and didn't want her marrying the likes of Bo Bo, an ex-con.

We were still living in the old Victorian house, and after the wedding and the party was over, when Jo came over to help clean up downstairs in what had been the casino, Pauline asked Jo how her dad was taking it.

"Actually," Jo said, "he's having a snit fit! But he'll come around. Right now, he thinks I've lost my mind."

"Well, Jo. Can you blame him?" Pauline said. "You guys didn't exactly have a long engagement."

"That wouldn't have made any difference. You don't know my father! He would never have accepted Bo Bo. My dad's one of those people that never gives in easily. Can he ever make it miserable on you if he doesn't like what you're doing. He freezes you out. You get the cold shoulder treatment. It's just as well we got married like we did. Anyway, thanks to you guys, it was so romantic." Jo said, raising her eyebrows and making goo-goo eyes.

Pauline and Mom started laughing. So did I. Jimmy and me were downstairs with them, eating some of the leftover cake while they were cleaning. At the party, Bo Bo had been telling everybody there how Jo swept him off his feet and how he couldn't resist her charms. He was acting like he was clowning, but you could tell he meant it. Jo was clowning around right with him. Mom said it was no wonder they fell for each other. One was as loony as the other!

Bo Bo kept calling Jo "baby" and "a dame." He said it like Humphrey Bogart did in the movies. Jo kept pretending she was Lauren Bacall. Mom thought Jo was sultry looking, like Lauren Bacall. I did too, so did everybody. She had this husky voice, like Lauren Bacall. Jo was really pretty. She had long blonde hair all down her back that she wore parted on the side, so it fell across one eye, and she was always having to push it back.

Only later, Bo Bo yelled at her about it.

"Christ, get that hair out of your eyes. You look like a damn sheepdog!"

That was afterward when he wasn't thinking she looked so sultry anymore. "When the 'glow' wore off," Mom said.

To spite him, she started wearing it all pulled back in a ponytail. He really started in then. She said that if he didn't shut up, she was going to get it all cut off. Boy, she would have done it! She had a hot temper like Bo Bo, and she wasn't even Italian.

When they weren't fighting, and he would be kidding around, he would always call her a *red hot mama*. When they were fighting, he would call her lots of other things. She would call them right back! What she called him mostly was a bastard.

She'd say, "that damn bastard."

I only heard her say it once. I thought Mom and Pauline were going to have a hemorrhage because Jimmy and me were there. Mom yelled at her for saying it in front of us. She apologized, but we knew she talked that way all the time when she got mad. She let stuff slip out when we were around. If we were there, and she was mad at Bo Bo, her eyes would get into narrow slits, and she would leave out words and mutter under her breath. Jimmy and me would try to guess what they were. It was pretty easy. I mean, it was mostly always the same thing —*bastard*, or *dirty s.o.b.*

Jo started coming over in the morning for coffee with Pauline. After we moved, everybody started coming over to our restaurant. A lot of the people who used to be at the club came. The police that used to raid the club, and the detectives, came in for breakfast or lunch. At night, on the weekends, they would come in like it used to be when the club was open. The difference was now it was legal. And they would often bring their wives and kids. It was like one big, happy family, Dad said.

Jimmy came over, too, or I would go over to his house. We still got to eat together sometimes. He would come over and eat lunch in the restaurant, on the weekends, or supper with me after school in a back booth if Mom was helping out waitressing. We would have malts, and shakes, and hamburgers. My mom made terrific chocolate milkshakes, and my dad made great burgers.

Our mothers started this bridge club. My dad said it was another way so the girls could get together and gossip, but he said it kidding like. My mom said the men did the same thing when they dropped in the restaurant for breakfast, and all crammed into a booth with their coffee mugs.

Jo started coming over more often later that year when Bo Bo and her weren't getting along. Mom said Jo needed somebody to talk to. The reason Jo was allowed to come was that Bo Bo still worked on the docks, like before he went to prison, only now he had an inside job doing paperwork. He still went to work early. Jo would drop him off, like Missy Greenburg did for my Uncle Ralph, and stop over to have coffee and kibitz.

It wound up getting Pauline and Mom in trouble. Bo Bo got mad at them for telling Jo stuff. It started an argument. He happened to drop over to Pauline's one day, to see if Big Jim was around when Mom and me were there. Jo was visiting her mother.

"Dammit, you two, I got enough problems without you filling her head with ideas. Damn bunch of women sitting around yakkin'. I don't want Jo working. That's my business, dammit!"

"Bo Bo, who do you think you're talking to!" Pauline said, "I don't appreciate being referred to as a *damn woman*. As far as putting ideas in Jo's head, she's not a five-year-old. She does have a mind of her own!"

"All right, I'm sorry, but dammit, Pauline, I'm tired of hearing it. I got married to have somebody to come home to. I want a wife. I don't make bad money. There's no reason for Jo to work."

"But Jo's used to working, Bo Bo. You don't have any kids yet. She's bored silly, being at home all day."

"Yeah, she's used to working for her old man in accounting, and dammit, she's not going back there! He'd love to rub it in my face that I can't even support his daughter. As for what she could do all day, she could try to learn how to be a wife, that's what! Christ, she burns everything she cooks. She can't even iron a shirt decent. I have to take them to the damn laundry!"

"Big deal, you took them there before you got married!" Mom said, putting in her two cents.

"Christ! I got married so I wouldn't have to!" Bo Bo said. "Well, if that's the only reason you got married," Pauline said, "you sure picked the wrong person. You mean to tell me you didn't know any of this before?"

"No, I didn't know! Okay, I knew she wasn't any great cook. But she said she could learn. She knew what I wanted. I'm not asking for any more than any other man would, Pauline. How do you think Big Jim would like it if you suddenly took a job?"

"Maybe he wouldn't be crazy about it right off, but it wouldn't be that big of a deal! Besides, you're missing something, Bo Bo. I have a job. Who do you think helps with the tenants? Keeps all the books straight? Sees that all the repairs are made? Listens to all the complaints? I don't just cook and clean! Fortunately, I happen to like most of what I do. But some women don't! Did you ever think that maybe Jo isn't cut out to be a housewife?"

"I don't give a damn if she isn't! She just better learn to be if she wants to stay married to me!"

So when Jo came over for coffee at the restaurant one morning, they started talking about it. All the women were together, no men were there, and Jimmy and me were sitting in the next booth in front of them, where we could hear. Now that we were older, they hardly ever made us leave. Mom told Jo maybe she better try to compromise.

"Look, Jo, at least learn how to cook for him. It's not that hard to make some basic meals. You can't eat eggs and canned soup all the time! If you could show Bo Bo you're trying, then maybe, you can talk him into you working part-time."

"God, I'll never learn! He wants me to make all the Italian stuff his mother made! Handmade pasta! I don't want to learn. I just hate it!"

"Then why in the Lord's name did you ever say you would?"

"Because I thought I might! I suppose I thought even if I didn't, it wouldn't matter. I thought Bo Bo was marrying me for who I was. I just thought he'd love me no matter what, even if I wasn't a great cook or a housewife. Talk about stupid!"

"I hate to say this, Jo," Aunt Betty said, "But you might as well learn now. Most men don't compromise. It's always the woman who has to if she wants to keep the peace."

"That's true," Mom said, glancing in Aunt Betty's direction, "but some men happen to be a little more flexible than others."

"You sure can say that again! Bo Bo's about as flexible as a brick wall," Jo said.

"Just don't forget," Pauline said, "Bo Bo comes from an Italian family. That makes one hell of a difference! I used to sit and listen to him talk about his brother and how it was when his parents were alive, and he was a kid."

"Yeah, you don't have to tell me! I've heard it about a billion times! He talks about his mother like she was a saint. I've had every meal she ever made described to me in great detail. How she was this wonderful cook and mother. How you could eat off her floors, they were so clean. It got so I hated her until I saw a picture of her older when we were in New York at Bo Bo's brother's house. She looked like something the cat drug in. Poor woman!" Jo said, rolling her eyes. "She probably died of exhaustion, instead of heart failure!"

"Oh Jo, you're terrible," Mom said, half laughing.

"Maybe you should have seen that picture before you got married?" Pauline said.

"Hell, I was so crazy in love, I'd probably thought that she was quaint looking, instead of plain worn out!"

"That sounds familiar," Aunt Betty said, "When I married Ralph, the stars in my eyes were so bright they could have lit up a Christmas tree!"

"I remember that," Mom said, looking at Aunt Betty. "Mother tried to talk you into waiting. Everybody tried to talk you into waiting, but then you weren't any different than anybody else. You were afraid Ralph would never come back from the war. Everybody was just trying to grab what happiness they could."

"I suppose so. The war certainly pushed more people into marrying faster, but I still think I would have been as blind. When I look back, Ralph wasn't so different then. I just saw him the way I wanted to see him. I can remember thinking how wonderful it was that he was so strong. If I couldn't decide about something, he just stepped right in and took charge! He was good at making decisions. I didn't see until after we were married that a lot of what it was, was to get his own way!"

"Yeah, that's what I missed with Bo Bo. You only see it in the best light," Jo said.

"It's because you're so in love. That is why they say, love is blind. You don't stop to think that if you're married to a man like that, you might be in for a lot of compromising!" Aunt Betty said.

"But there is such a thing as too much compromising!" Mom said. "A lot of times, you give in to Ralph, instead of standing up for yourself, Betty."

"I know it!" Aunt Betty said, shaking her head and looking down into her coffee cup with her mouth set.

"I mean, it's one thing to compromise, but it's another to be a doormat!" Mom said, starting to laugh. "I don't know a woman who doesn't compromise if she's married, but you have to draw the line somewhere!"

"Ralph is like Bo Bo," Jo said. "They expect you to be at their beck and call, Betty. And to do their bidding. Like with those damn dogs of yours. Bo Bo would be the same way. Ralph's the one that wanted them. You're the one that got stuck taking care of them."

"I know, but I end up just giving in because I can't stand to hear it! It's easier to do things than listen to him gripe, but that's changing, because I can't do it anymore. I don't have the stamina. I love those dogs, but he's going to have to help. And start picking up after them, and himself. My nerves can't take it!"

"At least you quit smoking," Pauline said.

"Now, if I can lose this extra weight."

"Well, if you put your mind to it," Mom said.

"Yeah, it's amazing what you can do. I never thought I would be able to quit smoking until I finally made up my mind. That was most of the battle. Even with Ralph, I used to think that if I made a fuss, I'd never hear the end of it! But I started to see that if I ignore it, he stops complaining after a while."

"If his complaints fall on deaf ears, he will." Mom said. "As long as you don't get weak-kneed and give in. Start sticking to your guns. Every time you don't, you get sick."

"I know the doctor warned me the last time," Aunt Betty said, shaking her head.

"You know you can do it, Betty. Like I said, stick to your guns!"

"Sometimes I wonder who's the weaker sex," Pauline said. "More often than not, it's the woman that has to be strong. Maybe, we start out having stars in our eyes, but at least we're able to see where we went wrong. Most men don't. What are they blinded by? Look at the whole thing with the club and Ben Beacon. Talk about bad judgment!"

"Well, it proves men aren't any better off than women are," Mom said.

"They like to think they are. Women are still more flexible than men," Pauline said. "They are not so invested in being right. I have no doubt that the guys wouldn't have closed the club if Ben hadn't killed an innocent customer in the club and damn near killed Tally. They'd have kept it open until they were closed down. It's like they refused to see that things weren't the way they used to be."

"It's more than that," Mom said. "It's more not wanting to admit they didn't have any control over things. I think that's what it all comes down to, especially for a man. Men have always had more control over their lives. It is women who have always had to do the adjusting."

"Oh, I believe that!" Jo said. "But women don't use it when they should, when they do have control. I didn't! A little bell went off when I first met Bo Bo. Like a warning. Only, I ignored it. I always know when I'm doing something that's going to get me in a heap of trouble. Every time I've ignored it, I've gotten clobbered. Most people get a warning. You just ask people. Over and over, you'll hear people, mostly women, say how they knew they shouldn't have done something, but they do it anyway!"

"That's true. But once you are in something, you have to learn to cope with it," Mom said.

"Well, I don't know if I can cope with this," Jo said. "Or even if I want to!"

CHAPTER TWENTY-FIVE

There was snow on the ground from the day before. There was blood splattered in it. Red blood that turned pink from the snow. There were tire marks where the ambulance had pulled up in the driveway and from the police cars. Jimmy kept staring at it, but I wouldn't look.

"Let's go," I said.

"Do you think she did it?" Jimmy said.

"Course not! It was an accident, like Mom said. She didn't even know how to use a gun!"

"All you have to do is pull the trigger!"

"God, you don't think she meant to kill her? She would never have done that! Mom said it just went off," I said.

"Oh, yeah! Then how come the police have her?" Jimmy said.

It happened before we got home from school, so we never saw anything but the blood. Aunt Betty drove up as we got back to my house. Pauline and Big Jim were at the hospital, so Jimmy was going to stay for supper, but it was too early yet. Mom and Aunt Betty went into the kitchen for coffee, and we went along. We had some of Mom's homemade chocolate chip cookies and milk while they talked.

"What did the doctor say?" Aunt Betty asked Mom as she sat down at the kitchen table.

"They're pretty guarded, but they'll know more by tomorrow," Mom said, pouring coffee, then looking at us.

"Why don't you kids take your milk and cookies and go in the living room to watch TV?" Mom said.

"We want to know what's going on," I said.

At first, I thought she was going to tell us to go in the other room, anyway.

"Well, I suppose you ought to know," she said, looking at the two of us and shaking her head like she was beside herself that she had to talk about it.

"I can't believe this happened," she said, shaking her head again. She tried to explain to us how it had to have been an accident.

After that, she changed the subject, and they started talking about Aunt Betty's new part-time job in a beauty shop where she had just started working. We knew there was more, but Mom didn't want to say anything in front of us. So after we finished eating, we went into the living room and turned the TV on, but later we went into the dining room, back where we could hear them. Sure enough, they were talking about it.

"Pauline says the bullet lodged in her throat," Mom said.

"Poor Pauline, I feel so sorry for her. She's going to be a wreck." Aunt Betty said.

"I know this sounds terrible, but I'm glad I wasn't the one that walked over there," Mom said. "I was busy helping clean up from the breakfast crowd downstairs when Beth called, asking if one of us could come quick. So Pauline went."

"What did Pauline say?" Aunt Betty asked.

"She said when she got over there, Jake was on the floor in

the living room by the cocktail table, making these horrible gurgling sounds, blood all over. She said she never went in the house any further than the kitchen. She said Beth was hysterical, screaming and screaming. Pauline said she had to shake her to get her to stop, so she could call an ambulance."

"God, what did she do until you got there?" Aunt Betty asked.

"Nothing. She wouldn't touch Jake. She couldn't do anything for her. The phone is on the wall in the kitchen with a chair under it. I guess Pauline shoved Beth into the chair when she called the ambulance, or Beth fell into it. Anyway, by the time Pauline hung up, Beth had slid onto the floor sobbing. So Pauline said she just sat down beside her. Beth was sobbing the whole time, holding onto Pauline, saying it was an accident, until the ambulance arrived."

"God!" Aunt Betty said. "It's like a nightmare!"

"I know. I can hardly stand to think of it. I can picture Jake on the floor. God, I can't believe this! And I'll never believe that Beth did it on purpose! That girl was deathly afraid of guns. She didn't even want one in the house. I keep running it through my mind, the night she came down here after Jake bought that gun. She was so upset."

"Why did Jake buy it in the first place?"

"Some woman was raped out at the plant, in the parking lot. She bought it to carry in the car. She wanted to take Beth out to the practice range and teach her how to use it. You know they both work late. I guess there had been a robbery out in the parking lot, too. But Beth wouldn't even talk about the gun. She told Jake to get it out of her sight. She never wanted to see it."

"So, how did it happen?" Aunt Betty asked.

"I don't know. I know they weren't getting along. Jake was running around. They had been having blow-ups over it. But I can't believe Beth could have shot her."

"You said they had Beth at the police station."

"I guess she's still there. I don't know. When Pauline called, they had just taken her," Mom said. "When the ambulance got to the house, Pauline and Beth went with it. Well, the police were called right away, I suppose whenever there's a shooting. I don't know who called them, ambulance attendants, or what, but I do know that they treated Beth for shock at the hospital. Pauline said she couldn't stop screaming and sobbing."

"When did the police take her?" Aunt Betty asked.

"I guess later, at the hospital, they questioned her. That's when they took her downtown. I don't know whether they booked her or not. Big Jim drove down to the station, and Pauline stayed with Jake. I have a feeling Pauline will probably stay up at the hospital with her all night tonight. The hospital called Jake's sister in Philadelphia, but she can't get here till the morning. I don't know about her mother. Her dad died a few years back. I suppose her mother will come."

"What about Beth?"

"Well, she has family, a brother, I think. I assume Big Jim will call them for her. I'm sure she'll be released!"

Only, she didn't get released. Early the next morning, Pauline called before I left to catch the school bus. Jake was dead, so they kept Beth locked up. Mom was standing in the kitchen with the phone in her hand, crying, was how I knew.

I kind of wanted to go to the funeral home. I couldn't imagine Jake being in a casket, dead. I kept trying to picture her that way, with satin all around her and her head on a satin pillow. Instead, I would start seeing her swimming around in the pool, or making jokes, or cracking her gum like she always did, grinning. I kept wondering what they would put on her to wear. I mean, she would look stupid in a dress, but you couldn't be lying there in satin, wearing one of those men's shirts and trousers she wore. I couldn't believe she could be dead. I told Jimmy, what if she wasn't all the way dead. If they revived her like a woman in a TV movie we saw.

"Yeah, only she's dead!"

"You want to go to the funeral home?" I asked.

"No, I don't want to see anybody in a casket."

"How come?" I asked.

"Because."

"Because, why?"

"Because they're dead!"

"But don't you want to see what she looks like? Even a little?" I asked.

"No, why would you want to see a dead person? It's creepy. Looking at their body. They can't talk, or see, or anything."

"But maybe their Spirit can see. Maybe their Spirit knows you're there." I said.

"Maybe, but I bet it wouldn't hang around. Who'd want to watch a bunch of people bawling over 'em. I wouldn't want a bunch of people staring at me, bawling." Jimmy said.

"God! I never thought of it like that. Wouldn't that be awful, having to watch everybody and not being able to say anything? Watch everybody being sad and not be able to tell people goodbye. Like maybe, you'd want to tell somebody something you forgot. Beth can't even say she's sorry. Jake would have to watch her cry."

"I think they should just bury people," Jimmy said. "Everybody go right to the cemetery."

Later, when the funeral was over, Penny Yarbrough came back to Jimmy's house with us. Pauline, Mom, and Penny were all out in the kitchen having coffee, talking about if Beth could have shot Jake on purpose. Jimmy and me listened from the living room. We knew they might not want us staying in the kitchen.

"I can understand how she might have done it," Penny said. "I know how I felt when Jake told me we were through."

"I can't imagine Beth doing it!" Mom said.

"Neither can I," Pauline said.

"I can! You have no idea what it's like to be in that kind of position," Penny said." I'm not a violent person. I can't even stand to kill a bug, but there were times that if I'd had a gun in my hand, I could have shot her. I was in such a rage. When you're dependent on somebody like that and, all of a sudden, they tell you it's over, that's it! Well, you get crazy. And from what I understand, Beth did about what I did. She built her whole life around Jake."

"From that viewpoint, you're right," Pauline said. "I know Beth hardly ever did anything without Jake. She consulted Jake on everything. I remember thinking one time, when Beth and I were out shopping, when they first bought the house and were decorating, how strange it was that Beth was going to ask Jake before she bought drapes she saw. She was like that with every-thing. She wouldn't do anything without asking Jake first."

"But how in God's name could you kill somebody you're that close to?" Mom said.

"Who said she meant to kill her?" Penny said. "I don't think she probably meant to kill her. I'd have never thought about *actually* killing Jake. As mad as I was at her, I didn't sit around thinking about shooting her. What I think happened was the situation got out of hand."

"When we were at the hospital before the police got there to question her, Beth kept telling me it was an accident," Pauline said. "I asked her where the gun had been. She said Jake brought it out in the living room from the bedroom, but she wouldn't tell me why."

"I can make guesses as to what that might have been about," Penny said. "When Jake was through with someone, she was through. She could be as cold as ice. Crying, threats, nothing worked! One time, when I threatened to kill myself, and she knew I was capable of it, from when I took all those pills when Jed left me, she handed me a butcher knife. She said if I was going to do it, do it outside. She didn't want blood on the carpet."

"Lord!" Mom said.

"That doesn't sound like Jake to you, does it?" Penny asked.

"No," Mom said.

"Well, you know what they say, don't you?" Pauline said. "You never know what goes on behind closed doors!"

"Yet," Penny said, "looking back now, I can understand. There are always two sides to a story. Jake got a little more than she bargained for."

"What do you mean?" Mom asked.

"Jake came along in my life when I needed someone. Which was great, except that it went too far. She sort of started running my life. I was a shy kid from a hick-town. I let her take over. Only the outcome was, I got more and more helpless, and eventually, she got fed up and wanted out. She couldn't stand it when I became a clinging vine. Yet, she helped make me that way."

"Sounds to me like that is a possibility of what might have happened between her and Beth." Mom said. "It's funny how some people keep picking the same situation to get themselves into. There's a saying about that. Some people have a thousand experiences, and others have the same experience a thousand times. Odd, isn't it?"

"Tragic is what it is," Pauline said. "Especially in Jake and Beth's case. But what keeps driving me nuts is wondering what went on in that room? What's strange is that Jake refused to tell the police anything before she died. The detective was furious. She could have. She was awake for a short while and was given paper and pencil to make a statement. She pushed them away, turned her head. I know she understood."

"I don't think it's so strange," Penny said. "Knowing Jake, even if Beth did shoot her, she probably knew damn well that it was half her fault that she pushed Beth. Plus, the last thing Jake would have wanted was to have to go to court. I don't have any doubts that if she had lived, she would have said it was an accident, even if it wasn't."

"Yeah, you're right there," Mom said. "God, she'd have been mortified at it being in the paper and everybody knowing!"

"All I can say," Pauline said, "Is that I hope Beth gets out of it. I'll never believe that it was anything more than an accident. She's going to have to live with it the rest of her life. That is punishment enough."

"Yeah," Penny said. "But a jury will look at everything. I don't think Beth meant to kill her either. Only the point is that if Beth picked up the gun and pulled the trigger, Jake is still just as dead, whether Beth meant to do it or not!"

"But if Jake provoked Beth," Pauline said, "Then it still wasn't entirely Beth's fault."

"No, but I see Penny's point." Mom said. "What it comes down to is that Jake is dead, and Beth is alive. So who do you blame?"

"Maybe that's just it," Penny said, "You can't necessarily blame one more than the other. I used to think that you could break it down that way. Either a person was right, or they were wrong. Situations aren't that simple."

Jimmy said that because Beth's fingerprints were on the gun, she was guilty.

"So who cares how come she did it, she just did it!" Jimmy said. "I suppose you think because Beacon was crazy, he shouldn't have gotten blamed for almost killing Tally and for murdering that other guy."

"You know I don't!" I said.

"It's the same thing," Jimmy said.

"It isn't either. Beacon was mean-minded, like a lot of people said. Even at the trial, they said he was," I said.

"But it didn't matter. He was guilty even if he was crazy," Jimmy said.

"But Beth wasn't crazy like Beacon. What I mean is that even if Beacon was crazy, he still didn't care if he shot somebody. He wasn't sorry!"

"Well, I say it doesn't matter why, even if she was sorry, she's still guilty like Beacon!"

"Well, I say she isn't! And I bet she doesn't have to go to jail, either!"

"Bet you she does," Jimmy said.

At school the next day, I asked Mr. Stanhope what he thought. I figured for sure, being so religious and fair, he would think the jury wouldn't find that Beth was guilty.

"That's a hard one, Caroline. It's hard to say what they'll decide," Mr. Stanhope said. "I'm afraid I'm a poor one to ask. I don't know a whole lot about jury trials, particularly this one."

"But what do you think from what I've told you? Don't you think they wouldn't find her guilty? Especially when the lawyer tells them how Jake handed her the gun? That's what Beth said happened. Jake pushed her into it!"

"I don't know, Caroline. I don't know."

"But what do you think? Do you think she's guilty? If a person shoots another person, are they still guilty even if it wasn't all their fault and they didn't mean to?" I asked, wanting an answer.

"Of what you're asking, it's not my opinion that matters, but the word of God. The answer to that is one of the ten commandments, *Thou shalt not kill*."

"But what about when someone is provoking? My mom said Jake provoked Beth to shoot her, and, besides, the gun went off accidentally. Beth said she didn't pull the trigger on purpose. It just went off."

"I imagine it's because they have to decide if Beth accidentally shot and killed Jake."

"How come then they have to know all this other stuff they are asking her? And what about someone like Ben Beacon, who I told you about, who killed that guy at my dad's club and went on trial. They were trying to say he was crazy, so he couldn't help it. Everybody already knew he did it on purpose. He knew it was wrong."

"Caroline, I can't answer all these questions for you, I simply don't have enough information, and above all, I'm not an attorney."

"So, what do you think happens to people like Beth, and like Uncle Tommy I told you about? He was drinking and hit two kids, but he didn't mean it. What happens when they die? They're not like Ben. They were good people. Do they get to go to heaven, or do they have to go to that purgatory place or hell?"

"The only thing I can tell you is that the Bible is the word of God. It's the highest law over what all humans do. The Bible says that all sins are forgiven by the Lord Jesus Christ, and through him, we are given everlasting life if we accept him as our savior."

"What if people aren't religious? Like Uncle Tommy didn't go to church. But he did a lot of good things."

"Well, that's not quite the same, Caroline. What the Bible means is that consciously, you have to take Jesus Christ in your heart and accept him as your savior knowingly. You have to be what is called, *saved*."

"But what if you're not?"

"You can't be forgiven for your sins, and you wouldn't be allowed into Heaven until Judgement Day. On Judgement Day, all sinners will be called into account and judged, and allowed a second chance for forgiveness from the Lord."

"But you'd have to stay and burn in hell that long, until then?"

"That's what the Bible says, Caroline."

I don't think I like that god much! I thought, wondering about other gods I read about. Maybe the Greeks ones weren't as bad. But I didn't say anything more to Mr. Stanhope.

Before the start of 6th grade, Beth got sent to prison for second-degree manslaughter. Ben Beacon just wound up in the crazy ward of a hospital.

CHAPTER TWENTY-SIX

Mom said I was old enough to start babysitting. I was supposed to wait until I was 12 years old at Christmas, but I got to start earlier as it was Alice's kids. Also, because Alice and Tally's house was close by. If I needed help, Mom could run over. Besides, the kids were always in bed sleeping when I got there. Michael was almost two, and Danny was eight months. Boy, were they cute kids. Michael looked like Tally, and Danny looked like Alice. Next, they wanted to have a girl. Alice was pregnant again. Mom said they sure didn't waste any time getting their family going.

Everybody was always teasing them about it, but it was good-natured. Everybody was so glad they were getting to have a family because of Tally getting shot and almost dying. I never believed he was going to die. I didn't care how many bad things happened. Some things were too awful to happen. If they ever did, it would be so horrible. Everybody would want to die too! That was what Alice said she would have done if Tally had died after he was shot. I think she would have. I wouldn't have blamed her one bit, either. I would have done the same thing.

Mona had yelled at her at the hospital, Pauline said, telling Alice she was going to lose the baby if she didn't quit going on like she was.

Alice said she didn't care! She didn't want to live without Tally and kept sobbing so hard.

Mona told her to stop it and think about the baby. That Alice wouldn't be alive if Mona had carried on the way Alice was doing when she was pregnant with Alice, and they told her Alice's daddy was dead.

Alice said she didn't want to raise a fatherless child. She would die first. The doctors had to give her a sedative. Later, they found out Tally was going to live, but he was sick for a long time. Alice said she didn't care. She would nurse him forever, as long as he didn't die. She said when he was still so bad, she kept having awful thoughts that a terrible dream she used to have was coming true. She said she wanted her life to be different from her mom's. When she was a kid, she used to have this bad dream about how she had this wonderful husband, and he died, like her dad. She said she was terrified that maybe her life was going to come out like Mona's.

Even after they knew Tally was going to live, they still thought Alice might lose the baby. She couldn't eat anything. She kept throwing up. She got dizzy, and the doctor made her stay in bed for weeks. It wasn't just worry over Tally, either. It was also because Mona had to go open her big mouth and tell Alice things she shouldn't have, Pauline said. She told her what nasty things Tally's Uncle William had said about her right after Tally was shot.

Pauline and Mom were so mad at Mona; they were ready to wring her neck. Mom said it was because Mona couldn't wait to say, I told you so, about Tally's family being so uppity.

Mona had gone down to the cafeteria to get something to eat with Alice, Mom, Pauline, Big Jim, and a few others.

They've been waiting up all night at the hospital to find out about Tally after they operated on him. Mona forgot her cigarettes and lighter in the waiting room, so she went back upstairs to get them. When she did, she overheard Tally's Uncle William talking to his Aunt Nadine. They were having an argument. Mona said she could hear them clear outside of the waiting room door.

Mona said Uncle William said he'd tried to like Alice but felt like a hypocrite. He told Aunt Nadine that if Tally hadn't married Alice, it wouldn't have happened. Tally should have married a nice, Catholic girl from a good family, like this sweet girl, Karen, he went with for a long time.

Aunt Nadine tried to defend Alice, but Uncle William said her family was the thing. He said that Alice didn't have a proper upbringing. She wasn't raised decent. Not like a good Catholic girl would have been. And converting wasn't going to make up for it. And all about Alice walking down the aisle and wearing a white wedding gown when she had been married before.

Aunt Nadine said the marriage was annulled. And that the dress wasn't white. It was light pastel. He said annulled, or not, when she married their Tally, he'd swear on the grace of God to it that she wasn't no virgin! And that it had come to no good. That their Tally would never have been in the devil's den if it hadn't been for Alice and her kind.

Mom said Mona came back downstairs and repeated the whole conversation, word for word. She was ranting and raving about how the whole family was nothing but a bunch of goody-two-shoes—and how Alice should never have married into it. Alice started bawling and went running for the ladies' room. Mom said Pauline got about as mad as she had ever seen Pauline get and exploded!

Mom said Pauline yelled at Mona telling her what she did

took the cake, and was one of the stupidest things to do, and why the hell couldn't she keep her mouth shut.

Mona started to yell back at Pauline, but wound up crying instead. Pauline brushed her off and went into the ladies' room to see if Alice was okay. Alice was in there getting sick. They had to get a nurse. After that, a doctor made Alice take medicine so she would sleep and stay calm.

When Tally got well, Alice told him what his uncle had said about her. Boy, did Tally blow up. Alice wasn't going to say anything at first. She told Mom and Pauline she thought maybe within time, Uncle William would change his mind about her. Except, Mona said that if Alice didn't tell Tally herself, Mona would. Alice said that wasn't the only reason she told Tally. Alice said she was fed up to the teeth with all their relatives, including Mona, her own mother, no less.

Mona was driving them nuts about wanting to leave Don and get a divorce. Jo had been talking about getting one from Bo Bo, and it gave Mona ideas. Alice said Tally and her were getting caught in the middle of family problems, and Alice wanted to put an end to it.

Although, what finally, she said, pushed her over the edge to tell Tally what Uncle William said about her, was him coming over to dinner after Tally got out of the hospital and acting awful to her.

When we went over to see Alice, she told Mom about it. "Oh, I don't mean that he was outright nasty. He is underhanded. That is what galls me more than anything."

"What do you mean?" Mom asked.

"When they came over, I wasn't feeling particularly well. I know he doesn't like coffee, and that was what the rest of us were having, so I asked him if he would like some tea. He said yes. So I made it. I was serving cake. I asked him if I could cut him a piece. He said yes. He never touched a thing. That wasn't the first time it happened, either. I've cooked whole meals, and he has just picked at them. Would make snide remarks, like the meat was a little dry."

"How infuriating," Mom said.

"Well, in the first place, he never liked me. I've always known it. You know that sort of thing. We had a lot of minor disagreements. Whatever viewpoint I took on anything, he took the opposite. If he disagreed with what I thought about anything, he would get this look of distaste. Like I disgusted him. What makes me madder is that even though I knew it, I kept trying. At times, he'd be nicer than others, and I start to tell myself, see, he does like me!"

"But Alice, people act in a lot of ways that they don't always mean," Mom said.

"No. He's never going to approve of me. That's the thing. If he doesn't approve of you, he doesn't like you either, especially if you happen to be a woman. If you don't share his opinion, then you're against him, rather than having a different opinion. Tally says it's even worse if your opinion happens to be right and his wrong. It's like he failed. To fail against a woman is the worst. Tally says it has to do with the old country and the church. The man is supposed to be the head of the household. A man always has to be right, or else, he's a failure."

"But Tally and you have a good marriage. That should count for something!" Mom said.

"I suppose that only makes matters worse because Uncle William doesn't understand. He doesn't understand that Tally and I can differ on things and still get along. Or that Tally could value my opinion. If you're married to a man like Uncle William, the only way is his way. If you're outspoken about your opinions like I am, he doesn't like it. Like, I should know my place. He doesn't trust women. Which is what took me a long time to see."

"You don't think he'll come around?" Mom asked.

"I'd be surprised. I think he's too stubborn. Tally left it up to him, but he made it clear, Uncle William has to start showing me some respect. Tally told Uncle William an apology was in order. Tally won't budge either. Neither one of us will. Tally and I have fought too hard to break away from that kind of thinking."

"I can't blame you there," Mom said. "You two want a big family. You don't want your children around a relative that treats their mother like a second-class citizen."

"For Tally, that is the crux of the matter!" Alice said. "He watched his mother die of cancer. He felt she gave up on account of the way his dad treated her. She was a smart woman. Tally's dad treated her like she was brainless. It's the same with Aunt Nadine. Tally said Uncle William brags about her college education and how smart she is to everybody when she's not around. Only, all he does it for is to build himself up for marrying such a smart woman. When no one else, except family, hears, he's always telling her how she doesn't know what she's talking about, cutting her down. Only, Aunt Nadine is stronger than Tally's mom was. She fights back! Tally's mom gave in until it destroyed her."

"How did Tally get along with his dad? I know he took over his dad's barrel company when his dad got ill." Mom asked.

"Tally said he loved his dad, but when his dad died, Tally felt for the first time in his life that he was free. He always did what his dad wanted, and he realized he was taking after him. Even though he didn't like the way his dad acted a lot, especially bullying his mother. He said he did a lot of thinking about it. He broke up with his girlfriend, Karen, over it. He said it hit him one night when they were out on a date. He said it was the oddest thing. They were in a restaurant. He said he looked over at her, and all of a sudden, he saw his mother."

"It must have scared him to death," Mom said.

"No, kidding! The same thing happened to me! It was when I ran off and married that guy. It was right before he left me alone in that dumpy hotel. We were broke, and he couldn't find a job. I didn't think he was trying very hard. He wanted me to get one first, like the one I had part time after school. We got in an argument, and as he turned in the doorway to leave, I saw Ernie! All I could think of was, my God, I'm with a no-count, too!"

"Alice, what are you going to do about Uncle William? You can't drop this!" Mom said.

"It's not like we're asking so much. I don't think an apology is out of line or asking him to start over. That's all we wanted was to talk it out and start fresh."

"But from what you're telling me, how can he do that? If he doesn't like you because of the way he sees things, how is he going to be any different?"

"I know. He won't even try! Aunt Nadine tried to talk to me. She called to invite us over for about the third time, even though Tally had told her no before, not until Uncle William calls and wants to talk himself. Well, her response was Uncle William isn't built that way. So there you have it. Which means I'd have to put up with his smart remarks and nastiness. Tally and I don't want to live our lives, or our kid's lives, subjected to that."

"Boy, that's rough, when it's Tally's only uncle." Mom said. "He's been like a father to Tally, helping him with the business and all. You need to think about this, Alice. Even if he is a jerk! Lord, honey, he's old. What if he dies, and you've been the one to keep them apart?"

CHAPTER TWENTY-SEVEN

Jo pounded her fist down on the table so hard all the coffee cups went clattering. I thought she broke her hand. "I'm so pissed I could chew nails! Greasy little bastard!"

"Oh, honey," Aunt Betty said.

"I never thought he'd run around on me. I should have known the bastard was running around," Jo said, starting to sob. "They always say the wife is the last one to find out!"

Pauline got her a Kleenex from her purse. And Mom poured her a fresh cup of coffee.

"Well, now you know why they say it," Pauline said. "So, what are you going to do?"

"Leave! That's what I'm going to do."

"Oh, Jo," Aunt Betty said, "you two haven't even been married that long!"

"So? It will put an end to this whole farce!" Jo said. "Maybe other women will put up with this kind of crap, but I won't! I won't take this from any man!"

"I don't know what to say," Mom said, shaking her head.

"I still can't believe the little creep had the nerve to tell me!

He tried to tell me that if I'd been the 'right' kind of wife, he wouldn't have had to get it elsewhere, the little bastard! I should have left to start with, instead of letting it drag on. I told him he didn't want a wife. He wanted a goddamn slave!"

A couple of weeks later, after school, when Mona, Mom, and me were at Pauline's, Jo came over. She said she had been to see this lawyer who was a friend of her girlfriend's husband. Jo said she started the divorce. She was moving out of the house on the weekend.

"Jerry, the attorney, wants me to go for alimony, but I told him the hell I would!" Jo said. "I'm not about to give the bastard the satisfaction of running around telling everybody how I took advantage of him."

"I sure would!" Mona said. "I wouldn't let Don walk off with everything."

"Yeah, but your situation is a little different. Besides, Bo Bo doesn't have a pot to piss in! He spends money like a drunken sailor. The only thing he has is the house. He can keep it! I never liked it anyway."

"Well, Don does, and I'm not going to live in poverty the rest of my life."

"Mona, are you thinking about leaving again?" Pauline sighed, sounding exasperated.

"I don't know. I know I can't go on forever like this. He drives me crazy. I never get to do anything I want. All-day long, I've got the house to take care of and meals to fix. The second he sets foot in the door, I've got to be right there. He yells, even if I'm only in the next room!"

"What's so bad about that? At least he's not out drinking or carousing around," Mom said.

"Yeah, hell, half the time, I couldn't even find Bo Bo!" Jo said. "He acted like I was violating a sacred rule by asking. Like it was a man's natural right to go where he damn well pleased.

A woman is supposed to stay home and keep the meals hot and the slippers ready. What a bunch of bullshit!"

"I know I shouldn't complain," Mona said. "But it's driving me crazy. I know you guys think I'm nuts! Here I am, with what sounds like every woman's dream."

"We don't either," Pauline said. "It's just you've got a better life than you've ever had. We hate to see you throw it all away."

"Have you tried talking to him?" Mom said. "I don't mean complaining or getting mad. But sitting down and talking to him? Letting him know how you feel."

"I've tried, but Don has his own beliefs about marriage. Don isn't like other men. Like Bo Bo and Big Jim, and Merle, for instance, they get together and play cards, talk. Or, even when it comes to us getting together with friends, other couples, Don doesn't care about any of that stuff. Remember, he's the one that talked me into going to a justice of the peace to get married. He didn't want a fuss. Even going to visit Alice and Tally, and the kids, he'll go, but it's just because he thinks we're obligated. It's not anything against Tally or Alice, either. That's how he is. How often have I gotten him to come over to the restaurant, like everybody else does, to socialize? Think about it!"

"Not often," Mom admitted.

"I used to think it was because he was shy," Mona said. "He'd never talk about it, or even give me an answer, if I asked why he didn't want to go someplace. When he isn't working, something always needs to be repaired around the house, or he is too tired. Always some excuse. The only place he wants to go is up north to the secluded cabin every chance he gets. If he had his way, he'd lock us in up there, and throw away the key!"

"But that doesn't mean you have to be that way, too!" Mom said.

"Oh, yes, it does! That's just it! He expects me to be right there. When he's home, I can't do anything. Even if he's going to be out working in the yard, I've got to be right there. He follows me around the house. My God, I can't even spend too long in the bathroom, or he's pounding on the door, wondering if I'm okay!"

"Well, for Lord's sake, speak up!" Mom said. "And if you want to go someplace, tell him you are going!"

"I can't! He pouts. He won't speak to me. I can't stand it!" Mona said.

"Then I don't know what to tell you," Mom said. "But I wouldn't put up with that!"

"You don't have to! Merle is not like that," Mona said.

"No, he isn't, but we have arguments. We don't always see eye-to-eye, but I'll be damned if I'll let him dictate to me."

"Well, I don't know," Mona said. "I don't know what I'm going to do. Don said if I ever left again, that'd be it. But, I can't stand living like this! Maybe I'll go see Jo's lawyer."

It was the summer, before Jimmy and me started the 7th grade that Jo came for breakfast at the restaurant to tell everybody she was a free woman. After she moved out of the house away from Bo Bo, she had only been over once since last winter. Only, we knew how she had been doing because Mona talked to her a lot on the phone. Also, Bo Bo had said some things about her dating the attorney who was working on the divorce. What he had to say wasn't so nice, but he was a sore loser, so Mona said.

Mona said the attorney guy sounded great, like he was more the kind that Jo needed, more responsible. Mom and Pauline didn't mention him, though. They figured when Jo was ready, she would tell them about him herself. They talked about the divorce. Jo said she was glad it was over.

"I guess if that's what you wanted, then I'm happy for you,"

Mom said. "But, I just feel bad that you two couldn't have worked it out."

"Some things you can't work out, Margie," Jo said. "Bo Bo makes a great friend. Give you the shirt off his back. He's a lot of fun. He made a great boyfriend! He wined me and dined me and treated me like a queen. The mistake I made was marrying him."

"We all make mistakes, Jo," Mom said.

"I know, but it still irks me. Bo Bo didn't turn out to be any better than my dad! He made my life just as miserable. With my dad, when I was growing up, I couldn't step out of line an inch. If I did something dad didn't like, there weren't any excuses in his book. I used to hate him for it. Bo Bo was the same damn way."

"What did your dad say about you leaving Bo Bo?" Pauline said.

"The usual I-told-you-so bullshit! How I should have listened to him in the first place. He didn't like Bo Bo from the start. But for all the wrong reasons. My dad thinks he has all the answers. He's always tried to run our family, like he runs the bank, with an iron fist."

"How'd your mom and brothers get along with him?" Pauline asked, curious.

"My mom went along with him. He was never home much when we were growing up. My mom left all the discipline to him. If we did anything wrong, she'd let him handle it. She took care of the house and socialized. She was always going to luncheons, or to some committee meeting, or giving dinner parties. He loved it. Everybody was always saying what a great little wife he had, so I suppose they got along pretty good. My brother, Ronnie, got along with him. Back then, I couldn't stand Ronnie, but I understood."

"How so?" Mom asked.

"Of my two brothers, Ronnie was the smart one. He put on a great act. Still does! He'd pretend like he agreed with my dad. It was like when I met Bo Bo. He was that way. He could get me to believe that he felt a certain way about something, but it would all be bullshit. Just to please me. That's how Ronnie was with Dad. In high school, he ran around with all these guys that had fathers that were big wheels. My brother and these guys drank like fish, and God knows what-all. They thought they were God's gift! My dad would never have believed it in a million years. Anytime Dad had an idea about something, Ronnie made Dad think it was brilliant! He was always buttering Dad up. Plus, Ronnie did enough of the right things, like getting good grades and playing football, to make Dad think he could do no wrong. But behind dad's back, he went out and did what he damn well pleased."

"Did your father ever catch on?" Mom asked.

"Hell no! Oh, maybe down deep, but he didn't want to see it. I'm the one that couldn't keep my mouth shut. Still, I don't think he was as furious at me as he was at my younger brother, Lloyd. Dad would fight with me. We'd get into screaming matches. He'd get so mad, I'd think he was going to have a heart attack. But poor Lloyd, sometimes Dad looked at him like he wished he'd never been born. I think that's why he never said anything about Ronnie. I think he secretly admired Ronnie's guts. Dad prided himself on being a man's man. One thing he couldn't stand was a sissy. Lloyd was the kind of kid that couldn't do anything right. He wasn't a jock like Ronnie. He got decent grades, but that was about all. He was scared of his own shadow. It drove Dad wild. He'd look at Lloyd like he wanted to smack the shit out of him."

After Jo left, when it was Mom, Pauline, and me, Pauline said she was sorry it didn't work out with Jo and Bo Bo, but it was probably for the best. She said they would never have been happy. They weren't right for each other. Bo Bo needed a woman that was content to be a homebody. Jo needed someone that would give her free rein and could afford a cook and house-keeper. Mom said, who knows, that maybe the attorney Jo was dating would be the one. I said I hoped she'd still come around, now that she wasn't married to Bo Bo any longer. Mom said she was sure we would see her once in a while, but not quite as much.

I was sure glad Alice and Tally got along. And Tally got well after being shot. Mom said they were the only ones that did really get *a happy ever after*. And they even worked it out with his Uncle William. Tally started to see his uncle alone, and Aunt Nadine would drop by to see Alice. When their first baby was born, Uncle William came to the hospital and brought flowers for Alice. That broke the ice. Now that they had three kids, they got along great. Mom said Uncle William had mellowed with age.

One night, a few weeks before school started, Jimmy came over when I went to babysit at Alice's house. I had been babysitting a lot, so I hadn't been able to be with Jimmy like most summers. Alice was helping Tally in the office during the day. Tally's secretary took the summer off to have an operation on her back, so I watched the kids. Sometimes I would watch them at night on the weekend, too, if Tally and Alice went to a dance or to play bingo at church on Fridays. They were playing bingo, and that was the reason I was going to babysit when Jimmy decided to come along.

It was the last night we were going to get to see each other. Jimmy was going to New York to stay with Uncle Tommy and Aunt Flo for three weeks until school started. Uncle Tommy had retired, but wasn't doing well. He had a stroke and was still recovering.

"You excited about being in the seventh grade?" I asked.

"Not really."

"I mean going to a bigger school and meeting a bunch of new kids?"

"It's just another school," Jimmy said.

"I guess I sort of think it'll be fun to meet some new kids."

"Maybe."

"I think it's kind of neat too, that we're going to be in junior high. Pretty soon, we'll be in high school. I can't wait," I said.

"Yeah. Dad said, as soon as I'm sixteen, I can have a car. That's only three years."

"You going to take me in it?"

"Of course," Jimmy said.

"I mean on dates?"

"Yeah! Sure!

"Do you think I'm pretty?"

"Yeah."

"I mean, really pretty?"

"Yeah, I think you're really pretty!"

"You think we'll still get married?"

"Maybe."

"You do not. You're just sayin' that."

"I do too. Honest! You're the one that probably won't wanna!" Jimmy said.

"I will too! Think we'll have lots of kids? I mean, like Alice and Tally? I think it'd be nice to have a boy and a girl. And have them close together like Alice and Tally. That way, they'd never be lonely, and they would have somebody to play with like we did when we were small."

"Only, we'd have to have four if we had more than two. Otherwise, a third kid would get in the way. Remember how Petey used to drive us nuts?" Jimmy said.

"Boy, were you glad when he moved away," I said.

"You couldn't stand him either!" Jimmy said.

"I used to feel sorry for him, though!

"I did too. Only, I couldn't stand him. God, was his dad a creep."

"Wonder what Petey is like now?" I said.

"Mom saw his mom at the dime store, and she said they were buying a house and were doing pretty good. Betcha Selma and Chappy are still fighting, though," Jimmy said.

"Maybe not. When people get older, they don't fight as much."

"Who says?

"Mom. She was talking one time about how when people get married too young like Alice did when she ran away with that guy, or like Chappy and Selma, how they sometimes fight a lot. They had too many responsibilities before they were ready. She said part of the problem with Chappy and Selma was that they were kids themselves when they had Petey. Do you think that would happen to us?"

"No! Chappy and Selma, or Alice and that guy, didn't know each other since they were kids like we did. Besides, I have to go to college first."

"I read a book about this couple that got married while the guy was still going to college. The girl got a job to help him, working at a candy shop like Russell Stover. I could write stories, or maybe a book, and sell it to help if you were still in college, and we got married."

"Yeah, but probably my dad would help us, too," Jimmy said.

Jimmy left before Alice and Tally got home from bingo. Tally always drove me home, even though it wasn't that far. Jimmy rode over on his bike. I walked outside with him when he got on it. He kicked the kickstand back.

"Be careful going home," I said.

"Yeah."

Then, he leaned across the bike and kissed me on the mouth. It was the first time he ever kissed me like that. I stood there for a while, thinking how nice his lips felt. I watched him ride off, getting smaller and smaller, thinking how great it would be when we were finally grown up and married. All evening, until Alice and Tally got home, I pretended I was waiting for Jimmy to come home. And that I was in our house with our kids.

CHAPTER TWENTY-EIGHT

The first day of junior high school was nothing like the way I thought it would be. Mom both made and bought me all new school clothes like she did every year, but this year, they were *teenage* clothes. The ones she made, we picked out of the Vogue pattern book, so I would be right in style. The first day, I wore a red and white checkered shirtwaist dress, with three red crinolines underneath, and white bucks, and bobby socks. Aunt Betty cut my hair in a pixie style, like Audrey Hepburn's was cut in the movie, *Breakfast at Tiffany's*.

Boy, was I ever nervous! The junior high school took in kids from three elementary schools, and I knew there would be many new kids. Sally, my friend, said that her older cousin told her how all the 8th-grade boys *look over* all the 7th-grade girls the first day. I was hoping nobody would notice me.

At study hall, where everyone from 7th and 8th grade went together, if you wanted to go to the library, where I wanted to go, you had to write your name on the blackboard with your homeroom number. I didn't want to have to get up in front of everybody, but my friends were going, so I did.

This boy named Donnie took down my name, only I didn't find out until after lunch. After eating, everybody went outside to walk around the school grounds. It was the perfect, warm, late summer day. I was out walking with Janet and Sally. Three boys that were 8th graders started following us. After a while, when we kept moving, it was pretty obvious they were following us. I thought they were doing it because they liked my friends.

Only, Janet said, "It's you they're staring at."

I thought she was nuts! Anybody could see she was the cutest, her and Sally. Janet started giggling, then Sally started. I told them to stop. I figured we should ignore the boys, hoping they would go away. There were about seventy kids standing around in small groups. Everybody started to catch onto what was going on. The guys were walking with their arms linked together like they were in a chorus line. They kept making wisecracks like, "Think they noticed us yet?" They were loud enough for everybody to hear. God, I could have died! Every time we moved, they moved. When we walked fast, they would walk fast.

Everybody was staring at us and snickering, watching to see what was going to happen. We stopped next to a large birdbath fountain in the courtyard. I told Janet and Sally to stare at the fountain, and maybe they would go away, but they came up right behind us. They stood there talking about us. Everybody started laughing.

"Hey, Caroline! Our friend here wants to meet you," one of the guys said.

"Yeah, Caroline, I want to meet you," this blond guy said.

"She ain't never going to turn around," one of the other ones said. "She probably thinks you're weird. Ha, ha! He's weird, Caroline. You don't want to meet him!"

"You creep! Don't listen to him," the blond one said, talking to my back.

"So, how do you know my name?" I asked the blond guy as I turned around, starting to laugh. I couldn't stand it anymore. They were elbowing each other in the ribs, and being so funny.

"I got it off the blackboard when you went to the library for study hall," he said with a grin.

"Yeah, he thinks you're cute, Caroline," the dark-haired one said.

"Yeah, he wants to ask you to a party," said the other guy.

"Will you creeps shut up! My name is Donnie Hall, and this is Mike Martin and Dean Allen."

"Hiya," Dean said, winking. "Sure you don't want to go with me instead?"

I ignored him, embarrassed, starting to feel dumb, probably turning red—not knowing what to say. The guy named Donnie, getting the hint, pulled his buddies, still all linked together, off in another direction, off to tease another group of girls. I thought they were joking about the party, but later the next day, Donnie wrote me a note and passed it to me in the hallway between classes. He asked for my phone number.

Boy, did I ever feel weird giving it to him. When he called, he asked me again to go with him. It turned out my dad knew his parents from them coming into our restaurant. And also, from all of them going to the VFW Post to dances. Donnie had his dad call my dad and tell him that he was chaperoning the party, as it was at Donnie's house, so it was okay. The plan was for my dad to take us to the party, and for Janet's dad to pick us up.

It was my first teenage party. We had a dance for 6th-grade graduation, but that was with kids we had known forever. So it wasn't any big deal like this. Mom made me a new dress with an empire waist. It was light pink with light brown bubbles all over it, and I wore three pink crinolines, with pink satin edging underneath, and nylons with brown flats.

Donnie kept telling me how great I looked, but I felt so silly. I wished he would stop. The party was neat! Donnie Hall was a sharp guy! We played 'spin the bottle,' and I kissed Donnie seven times. Every time I had to kiss Mike, a guy that was sitting next to a girl named Joanna, I kept thinking he had peanut butter breath. I told her when we were in line to use the bathroom.

"It's because he's been eating Reese's cups, silly! Didn't you see them in that bowl on the table?" Joanna said. Then afterward, she told everybody. Boy, did they get a charge out of that! Everybody started calling Mike peanut butter lips.

The guys had Donnie's basement decorated neat! They hung balloons and streamers from the pipes on the ceiling, and we had pop and chips. Donnie was a neat dancer. He could really dip. Everybody said we made a cute couple. He had a good voice, too. When they put on the song *Silhouettes* and we slow-danced, he sang it to me. He kept putting his arms around me and kissing me when we were dancing. Nobody noticed much, though, because there were colored bulbs in the lights, and it was sort of dark. Anyway, everybody else was doing it, too. God, was he sharp!

I took some Reese's cup wrappers home and the napkin that Donnie had his glass sitting on to put in my scrapbook. I wrote the whole thing in my diary. After that, Donnie started writing me notes at school. Everybody knew we liked each other. Donnie was a pretty big deal. Mike and Dean, and all these guys he ran with were sort of in this click that was the *in-crowd*. They were sharp dressers, the cool kids that everybody liked. They were all 8th graders. They introduced me to some other kids who were in their crowd. All of them had come from one of the other elementary schools. Not kids I'd grown up with, new kids. There were about thirty of us that hung out together.

Most of the guys played football, or wrestled, or played baseball. The girls were real cute. Donnie asked me to go steady, to be his girl. I thought I'd die! He gave me his ring to wear, and I wound pink angora around the inside back of it, so it would fit. He gave me half a heart to wear on a necklace, and he kept the other half. Neat! Neat!

The only thing was that I felt kind of weird around Jimmy. He never said anything about it. It was his own fault. He hung around with the smart guys like he always had. And he was always going bowling. I mean, he was really good and all. The guys he hung with were on a team, and they were winning all these tournaments. It was really cool, but he didn't care about meeting any new kids, or any parties, or anything. "So what" or "big deal" was his attitude. All he ever said was, "That's nice." I told him about Donnie asking me to his party. I mean, he could have said he didn't want me to go!

So when Donnie and I started going steady, I never mentioned it to him. He knew anyway. It was in the school paper. Everybody could see I was wearing Donnie's ring. Jimmy never said anything, so neither did I. We still sat together on the school bus when we got closer to home after most of the other kids got off.

Our junior high was a lot farther away from our house than grade school had been. It was a long bus ride. We were almost the last stop. Usually, I would go sit back by him. He mostly sat at the back of the bus. Sometimes, after my girlfriends got off, and the bus was almost empty, we would sit in the back, each of us in separate seats, but in the same row across the aisle. With the back of our heads resting against the windows and our feet sprawled out on the seat, talking until it was time to get off.

We never talked about school, except he might say some-

thing about Lester or a bowling tournament. I might say something about somebody he knew. We talked about people like Bo
Bo, or Alice, or Tally, their kids, or something. Like if Mona had
been over to the restaurant, I'd say, "Guess what, Mona was
over." Then we would talk about that. Or our moms or dads or
holidays, or I'd say he looked nice if he had on a new shirt.

Once, when Aunt Betty gave me a poodle cut and a permanent wave, my hair turned green from this black rinse I put on
it before the permanent. I was having a fit, but Jimmy said it
was pretty anyway. He said I always had pretty hair, and not to
worry. It would wash out.

"But God, it's green!"

"You can hardly tell. It's still so soft," he said, reaching over
to touch it.

A lot of times, we would just sit next to each other, and not
say much, or we would watch the farms go by. Maybe, one of us
would say how neat everything looked, talk about the leaves
turning color in the fall, or the snow on the ground. Just dumb
things.

By eighth grade, I broke up with Donnie. I still liked him all
right, but as a friend. I was going with this guy named Bill
Mason. Nobody went with anybody longer than a school year.
Mostly, everybody went with someone for a couple of months
until they started liking someone else.

Was Bill Mason ever sharp! All the girls were nuts over
him. He had dark hair and blue eyes, and he was a good kisser.
He went out for wrestling, and he had huge muscles. God, was
he so cool! Only, I didn't go with him very long. What
happened was it all got messed up. I started liking him first, and
by the time he started liking me, somebody else started liking
me. It was Mike.

See, I knew Mike kind of liked me. Every time I would be
someplace, he would wink at me, or say something cute. All my

girlfriends started saying he liked me. At the same time all this was going on, I started kind of liking a guy named Vince, but I was just getting to know him. He wasn't in our group, and Bill was sort of barely acting like he liked me. He only walked me to my class a few times.

Mike was sharp, though, too. So I was stuck! But that didn't last long, anyway. After that, I started liking a different guy for a while, named John.

School got better by the time I was a "frosh." I was having fun! Plus, I got the best teacher I ever had. Her name was Mrs. Bernstein. She taught history. The thing I liked about her the best was that I could talk to her. She wasn't one of those people that went around judging people. You could probably have told her the worst thing in the world, and she wouldn't have acted snooty. Another thing about her was that her husband had also been a teacher before he retired. Every summer, they traveled all over.

She was a reader like I was. We liked a lot of the same books. I always took a lot of books out of the library, and that was how we got to talking. It was a couple of weeks after school started. After her class was lunch period. Well, when the bell rang, I was slow getting up. I was reading something. Almost everyone else was gone. She noticed I had this huge stack of books. I had stopped to talk to someone before class, and I didn't have time to take them to my locker.

"Ten library books!" she said. "My, I guess you like to read, don't you?"

"Yes."

"*Anna Karenina*? Shakespeare? Pretty impressive stack!"

The second she said something, I started kicking myself for not getting to my locker. I wasn't what you could call any great student. I figured right away she was going to say something about my having so many books to read. How would I have time to study? Instead, she acted cool about it. Like it was wonderful. I couldn't believe it! After that, we would talk about books after class. Which was why I finally told her about my writing.

"Oh, how long have you been writing?"

"Ever since I was a kid."

"Do you have anything you might let me read?"

"I have some things. It's that they are not great. I'm probably not that good. Plus, I'm a terrible speller."

"Caroline, stop worrying. I'd be very honored to read them."

I gave her a couple of things. I gave her part of a novel that I had started, but what she liked the most was a story I wrote about Jake, titled "Heaven Waits."

"These are really good!" she said after she read them. "Especially this one, 'Heaven Waits.' What a beautiful story about forgiveness and love."

"You really think so?"

"Yes, I do! Caroline, I'm quite serious about this. You do have talent."

Mrs. Bernstein was great. I loved history. It was a neat school year, and in the summer, before my sophomore year, I had a blast! I liked about four different guys. We had parties every weekend at this park called Pearson Park.

A few of the guys had motorbikes, and everyone would take turns riding. Naturally, somebody always got thrown in the park pond. One time, one of the guys accidentally rode his bike in with two girls on it. What a riot! Usually, though, we mainly horsed around, and everybody went into the woods and *made out*. We girls made sure we stayed close, though, by another couple, so our guys didn't get too carried away, if you know what I mean. Only, girls that weren't *nice* girls let that happen. There wasn't any light among the trees, and it was pitch-black, and you could imagine anything you wanted, so romantic. It was like being lost in a forest.

Sometimes, if we weren't having a party at Pearson Park, we would have one at somebody's house. If there wasn't a party going on, there was always a hop. One of our fathers would take a bunch of us girls, and someone else's dad would pick us up.

I wasn't allowed to car date until I was sixteen. My father said no, I was too young. He had this little talk with me. I started crying and ran to my room. He came and knocked on the door. It was over this whole thing about going steady. Car dating. We got into this kind of argument. I didn't understand why he was upset with me. I wasn't doing anything wrong. He came in and sat down next to me on my bed. He started rubbing my back and talking to me. He told me he was sorry I was so upset.

"I know you're having a good time. And I'm glad you're so popular. Only, life isn't one big party. I know you think I'm being mean, but I want you to slow down. Right now, all the older boys with the cars, the handsome ones, the jocks—they look good. But there are more important things than outward appearances. Always remember one thing—all that glitters isn't gold."

About a month before school started, Mom and Dad let me go out with this guy on my first car date, even though I wasn't sixteen yet. Bob Rossford had been coming over to my house to see me. He was going to be a senior. Mom thought he was pretty impressive. Dad liked him, too. He always shook hands with dad when he came in. He was the kind of guy that parents would naturally like. He was polite, but he was always joking and kidding around, and he would always include my parents. He wouldn't come in and try to get me off alone. He would sit out in the kitchen with them and talk and eat my mom's cake. He wasn't putting on either, trying to make himself look good.

He was just like that. He asked Mom and Dad himself if he could take me out. He didn't leave it up to me to ask. He told them he knew I wasn't supposed to car date until I was sixteen. He told Dad he would take good care of me. He would make sure he had me home by my eleven o'clock curfew.

He was a swell guy, and we started dating all the time. After a while, he asked me to go steady, and I started wearing his class ring. Then, I guess I did about the dumbest thing I ever did. My girlfriend had been telling me about this sharp, sharp, looking guy that was a best friend of the guy she was dating. These were guys from a rival high school. I didn't know either of them. Sally had been trying to get me to meet this guy since before I ever started going steady with Bob, but it never worked out. I finally met him at a teenage hop that Sally and I went to near her house. Her dad dropped us off and picked us up. The guy's name was Butch Hall, and I danced all night with him. We hit it off big. At the end of the evening, he asked me out.

I knew I had to give Bob's ring back. I tried calling him, but he kept coming home and then leaving again. I kept missing him. The last time I called, his mom said he was shopping at the small strip mall shopping center, not far from my house. Sally's older sister had dropped her off to spend the day with me, so we walked over to the center and found his car in the parking lot. I left a note on the seat and his ring in the glove compartment.

God, I knew it was a crummy thing to do! I felt like a creep later. I knew he had to work that night, but the next morning, he called.

"So what's the beef?" he asked.

"I tried to get a hold of you. I talked to your mom." I said.

"Yeah, that's what she said. I want to know why you did it?"

"Wow. I'm sorry. It was a crummy thing to do."

"How about if I come over and we talk about it?"

When he came over, we went to the park. All the way over there, he didn't say a word. Nothing! He didn't even turn the radio on. I would have rather he had told me to drop dead on the phone like most guys would have. I knew he was mad, but he was so mature about it. I felt like a dumb jerk that had pulled some stupid kid prank. The worst thing was that I cared about him. I didn't know how much either, until we were driving along toward the park, and every time he would glance over at me, he would wince like it hurt. He was a nice guy who didn't deserve what I did, but I still had to tell him I couldn't wear his ring anymore.

When we got to the park, he pulled the car off the side of the road and shut the motor off.

"So, what did I do?" He asked.

"Nothing! It's all my fault, I guess, I just don't want to go steady."

"So why did you take my ring?"

"I liked you," I said, trying to explain. "I still do. But I guess it feels too serious."

I didn't want it to be that serious! Ever since I started liking guys, it always had been for fun. Everybody kind of knew it wasn't like you were going to be together forever, or anything, even if you're going steady. Hardly anybody stayed with the same person long. Everybody was always going steady and breaking up and going steady with somebody else. It wasn't like you were going to wind up getting married. For God's sake!

After Bob, I learned my lesson. No more going steady or taking some guy's ring. I liked Butch for a short while. Only, I dated other guys too.

I just wanted to have a good time!

CHAPTER TWENTY-NINE

After school started in September, our sophomore year, Jimmy started dropping over after supper, or else I would go over there, except on the weekends when I went on a date or to a party with my friends. We didn't do anything special. We would usually play cards or watch television. Then I found out he was going steady with this girl, and he never even told me. So I asked him about it when we were on the bus coming home from school.

"I saw Lester today at lunch, and he said you were going steady with some little freshman named Linda. How come you never said anything?"

"Well, it just happened a while ago."

"Still, you could have said something! I didn't even know you liked anybody."

"I didn't think you'd be interested. You never told me about anybody you ever went with!"

"You knew about Donnie Hall, the first guy I ever went with."

"You never told me. I found out from Lester. He said you were going with some big deal eighth-grader."

"But you never said anything. I told you about Bob. You could have said something."

"What was I supposed to say? You were always acting like it was the best thing that ever happened."

"So maybe it was! You never seemed interested in parties! You acted like it was dumb. Like it was silly or something. You were always studying."

"Yeah, well, maybe I'm a little more interested in my future than some of those jocks you hang around with!"

"That's not fair! A lot of those guys are honor students. You're just jealous!"

"Jealous! Jealous of those jerks?" He said, angry.

"Oh, brother! You think you're so smart." I said, getting mad.

"You're damn, right! Just because you live in some kind of fantasy—all you ever did was write in that journal of yours!"

"Oh, so now my writing's stupid, too! Thanks a lot!"

"I don't mean that."

"You know what it is? You don't trust anyone, Jimmy. You never have! You always think the worst." I said.

"So, all you do is run around thinking everyone's so great, everyone's so neat! That's all you ever talk about is how neat everything is! How cool everyone is!"

"Well, a lot of kids are cool," I said.

"Yeah, boys, you mean," he said, not looking at me and getting up because his stop to get off was coming up.

The next morning, when he got on the bus, he barely glanced at me when he went down the aisle past me, but on the way home, after almost everyone got off, he came up and sat down next to me.

"Hi," he said, hardly looking at me. "Are you still mad?"

"No, are you?" I asked.

"No. Why don't you get off at my stop, and I'll walk you home later?" he asked.

Pauline was making cookies when we came in, but they weren't quite ready yet, so we went to Jimmy's room. He showed me his new chess set. Neither one of us was saying anything about the argument. Finally, I couldn't stand it anymore.

"I'm sorry about yesterday," I said.

"Me, too," he said, not looking at me, as we both got quiet.

"How come you never said anything about the guys I went with?" I asked.

"I don't know," he said, shrugging and still not looking at me.

"I guess I kept hoping you'd say something," I said.

"What could I say?" he said, staring out the window. "I'm not like those guys, and all those kids you started running around with, I'm not one of the *in-crowd*. So what was I supposed to say? It was pretty obvious that's what you wanted. Once you started hanging around Donnie Hall and his gang, things changed."

"I didn't think you cared! That's why I never asked you to any parties. I wanted to have fun. I'm sorry." I said, feeling crummy, knowing I could have included him.

"Well, maybe I do want to have fun, too," he said with a grin, looking a little devious. "Why don't you go see if Mom's cookies are done and bring us some," he said.

"Sure," I said, getting up and heading for the door, wondering what he was up to, knowing that look he was wearing so well, and that it usually meant he was scheming.

Boy, was I right. The second I put the plate of cookies down —the squirt gun came out! Jimmy started laughing, and the chase was on! I got wet, but I didn't care. I knew when he walked me home, we were back the way we had always been with each other. Except, that this was going to be different. We weren't little kids anymore.

The next day after school, he got off at my bus stop to get a haircut. He always got one right down the street from my house.

"How about if you walk down to the barbershop with me?" he said.

The wind had started to blow, and it was gloomy out, the way it starts to get in November. You knew it was right before winter would take hold when it would warm up during the day, the sun coming out for a short while. Then, it would be cloudy and colder by the end of the afternoon.

"Think it might snow?" I said, shivering.

"Nah, it's not cold enough yet," Jimmy said, looking at the sky. "It might, but probably not. It could sleet, though. Boy, I can't wait until I get my license so I can drive instead of having to mostly bike or walk everywhere."

"Think you'll get a car for your birthday?"

"Hope so. Dad knows that's what I want."

"Can you believe that we're going to be sixteen soon and that we only have two more years of high school left?"

"I'll be glad to get out, too," Jimmy said. "Looks like I'll go to Ohio State, at least until law school, then I'll probably go to New York University where Uncle Tommy went."

"Yeah, walk faster. I'm freezing," I said, as I linked my arm through his, with our heads down against the wind. He matched his pace to mine.

"I hope I can be half as good as he was before he retired."

"Why? You're as smart as he is!" I said.

"Well, he was a smart attorney," Jimmy said, glancing at me out of the corner of his eye, grinning. "When he handled a case, he knew everything, I mean everything, by the time he was done. He never got rattled. Aunt Flo said when he was in court, he was as cool as ice. Nothing shook him."

When we got to the barbershop, boy did it ever feel good to get inside. It wasn't a very big barbershop. There were only three chairs so I could sit right in front of Jimmy and watch. Jimmy had been going there ever since we were kids, but I didn't think that the guy that cut his hair was such a good barber. I was looking at a magazine, but kept glancing up every once in a while. The guy was cutting it too short. Jimmy wore a flat top, but the barber was taking too much off the sides.

When we got back outside, I told him it looked nice, anyway. I figured once he got his driver's license and could find another barber, I would tell him then, no sense in making him feel bad now.

On the way back home, Jimmy was still talking about Uncle Tommy. I knew Jimmy was going to make a great lawyer. Everything that he said about Uncle Tommy was the way Jimmy acted.

"I don't know why you think you won't be as good as he is," I said. "You're just as smart, and you never let things bother you. I mean, you don't show that they do."

"Thanks."

We walked for a while without saying anything. It was almost too cold to talk. I kept wishing he wasn't going to Lester's to play cards. He had been playing cards with a bunch of his buddies for a couple of years. It wasn't very far if he took a shortcut by following the railroad tracks next to his house, and one of the guy's parents always drove him home.

"Okay, God, you're gonna freeze," I said, noticing how dark and gloomy it was getting.

"No, I won't. Go on and run to the house!"

As I started to dash off, he grabbed me and kissed me—a grownup kiss and held me tight.

I went to bed thinking about seeing him so differently. Before, he seemed so much younger. He had gotten taller over the summer. I always knew he was smart. At first, the other boys I hung around with, starting in junior high, seemed so much older than him, now they didn't. They were a lot of fun, but I knew Jimmy was who I always wanted to be with all along.

I drifted off to sleep, wondering what was going to happen next. As I slept, I had a dream of Jimmy and me as kids, but it was all jumbled up and turning into a nightmare. The dream woke me up in the middle of the night. It was so real. Not like a dream. The next thing I knew, I was running through the living room to the kitchen. Mom was on the phone. Dad was sitting beside her with his arm around her.

"Oh, God, Pauline, Oh, God! We'll be right over," she hung up the phone and looked at me.

"Jimmy is dead," I said. I don't know how I knew. I just knew.

They found Jimmy along the railroad tracks. The police came to tell Pauline and Big Jim. They did not suspect foul play, the police said. It turned cold, and he must have jumped for the back of a train to get home faster. The trains moved slower from where he jumped on, at a road crossing, to in front of his house, right before another crossing. It had rained, then frozen. They figured he slipped and fell under the train. He was decapitated.

Mom and Dad went over to be with Pauline and Jim for the rest of the night. I went back to bed. I don't think I was totally awake. Maybe I didn't want to be. The next morning, I got dressed for school, because I couldn't believe it was true. When I was ready, I got my books and went into the kitchen. Mom and Dad were at the kitchen table. Mom was smoking a cigarette, and her hands were shaking. All the time she talked, I kept watching the cigarette shake and the ashes falling on the table, making this little pile.

"Caroline, are you okay to go to school?"

"Yeah."

"Are you sure?"

"Yes!"

When I got outside, it was cold and ugly. There wasn't any sun. It was damp. It was as if nothing had changed, like it was yesterday, instead of today. I shouldn't have gone to school. It was only when the school bus came to the railroad tracks, and I saw the yellow tape, like they have for crime scenes, still hanging from one of the cross gates, that I thought it might be true. I still didn't want to believe it. Nobody talked on the bus.

Once I got to school, all the kids were talking about Jimmy being killed, and a lot were crying. A lot of the kids, especially the crowd I hung out with, weren't kids we grew up with, just new kids I'd known for a couple of years. They didn't even know I knew Jimmy other than we were both sophomores. I don't remember much of what happened, but I wanted to go home. One of my friends, Mary, and another one helped me down to the dean's office, then Dad came and got me.

On the way home, Dad stopped at the drug store and picked up some medicine that Mom gave me when we got home. I fell asleep for what seemed like a few days. I don't remember much, sort of eating and sleeping. A few days later, when I was waking from a nap, Mom cracked my bedroom door open a little. Noticing that I was awake, she came in and sat on the bed, and took my hand.

"Honey, I have to talk to you about something. Now, I want you to think about this before you answer. You don't have to go. Aunt Betty is coming over, and we're going to the funeral home. Tomorrow is the funeral. You don't have to go at all."

"No, I'll go."

"You sure, honey?" she said, giving me a worried look and patting my hands, holding them in hers.

On the way to the funeral home, Aunt Betty and Mom kept talking and talking. All I could think was how I wished they would be quiet. Aunt Betty was driving, and I was in the middle, so they had to talk around me. They would have stopped if I had asked them, but I didn't feel like saying anything. What started to bother me most was I kept thinking that what they were saying should mean something, but it didn't. I didn't feel anything.

"Lord, my heart goes out to Pauline. How do you think she'll hold up?" Aunt Betty said.

"I don't know," Mom said, putting her arm around me, pulling me close. "Last night, when I was there, and we were all sitting around the kitchen table, her arms were on the table. She was shaking so bad the whole thing shook. Coffee cups were ready to slide off, and she never noticed."

"The poor woman! I can't imagine. Has she cried?" Aunt Betty asked.

"Not so much. You could tell she had been crying earlier, her eyes were swollen, but it is all inside. She didn't even realize what she was doing, until I couldn't stand it anymore, and took her arms off the table. Big Jim wanted to call the doctor, but she refused. She said she wasn't taking anything. She'd be okay."

"How's Big Jim?"

"Bad. He had to go down and formally identify the body. He kept shaking his head and talking about the new car he bought to surprise Jimmy on his birthday. He kept talking about what a good boy Jimmy was. What a good son. You know Big Jim has never been one to do a lot of talking, but it was like he couldn't stop. God, the look on his face, it cut you to the quick!"

When Aunt Betty swung the car around the corner and into the parking lot next to the funeral home, I felt strange, like it wasn't really me sitting in the car. I don't remember getting out of the car and walking to the door.

The next thing I knew, I was standing on the inside of the funeral parlor, and Bo Bo and Pauline were walking toward me. Then I was backing up, trying to get back out the door. They were on both sides of me, pulling me inside, toward a room where I could see an open casket.

I kept saying, "No! No!" It didn't sound like my voice. I could see myself going through the whole thing, watching like I was outside of myself. I could also see the "me" that was watching, so I was sure it wasn't real. The person that was me watching wasn't supposed to go near the casket. I needed to leave!

"Caroline, don't be afraid, honey. There's nothing to be afraid of," Bo Bo said, talking soft, pulling me toward it.

"C'mon, honey!" Pauline said.

"No! No! Please, no."

"He looks so peaceful," Bo Bo said, forcing my head up. "Don't turn away. Honey, just look!"

It was Jimmy. He was dead. He was lying in a coffin. He didn't look strange. He looked like Jimmy. He looked the same way he always looked. Except, he was dead.

The only thing that was different was that his head looked all scrunched into his shoulders. That was probably because his head had been cut off under the train wheels, I thought.

Otherwise, he looked the same.

I would have preferred it if he had looked less like himself. The thing was, he looked too much like himself to be dead. I kept looking down at him and thinking that over, and over, and over...

He was wearing a navy-blue suit and tie and a white shirt. His hands were folded neatly across his chest. Everybody kept saying how peaceful he looked. There were beautiful flowers everywhere in the room. They were real. Only, they looked fake, and they smelled fake. Every time someone walked up, they would say how peaceful he looked.

I walked away a few times and came back to see how I felt each time. I reached out and touched his hands. I always thought he had beautiful hands. His fingers were long and tapered, and his nails always looked so perfect. When I touched his hands, they were cold. I kept staring at his head, remembering how yesterday the barber had cut his hair too short. If you looked close, you could see cuts on his scalp that the morticians tried to cover up with makeup. I started wondering what Jimmy would think about how he looked.

I knew exactly what Jimmy would say. Jimmy would say he looked dead. Not peaceful. He would say that the morticians made him look peaceful. He would say that people wanted to think he looked peaceful because it made them feel better. Jimmy would say that the truth was, he didn't die peacefully. He died horribly. Only nobody wanted to think about the truth.

I did not want Jimmy to think I was one of those people. Maybe, there was a chance that his spirit was still in the room. I wasn't sure, but I felt, somehow, if I talked to him, he could still hear me. So, I waited until there was no one else around, and then I went back up to the casket.

"God, Jimmy, I hope you can hear me. I love you, Jimmy. I keep thinking about all the things we were going to do. How stupid I was with other boys. I know I've let you down. I'm so sorry. I wish I could make it up to you. You were always trying to tell me. I always thought that somehow you could make things come out all right. Even now, I keep wanting to pretend you're not dead. I keep wanting to wake you up. Did it hurt? Did you feel anything? They said it happened so fast you never felt anything. They said you must have slipped—it was icy. I can't believe you jumped a train. I know you'd say, 'It was my own dumb fault.' God, you used to hate it when I'd start in about how someone couldn't help it. How they weren't to blame. I don't know why I never saw things like you did."

How could I still be alive, and Jimmy was dead? I never believed that anything so terrible could happen. Only, Jimmy always knew. Jimmy always knew that was why you had to be brave. If you weren't brave, you would be like most people—people who ran around pretending things weren't as bad as they were, or else complaining all the time, or worse, whining and blubbering about everything.

The day of the funeral, the sky stayed overcast. It rained off and on. It was an ugly rain. I hated it. The wind blew and blew. The rain would turn to sleet, then back to rain, then sleet again. If Jimmy were alive, he would have hated it as much as I did, probably more. He was right about believing that people shouldn't have funerals. On the way over to the cemetery, I kept thinking of that. I kept watching the windshield wipers and the rain splash against the window and thinking how Jimmy would hate it. It was quiet in the car. Aunt Betty was driving again. It was Mom, and her, and me. Dad took our car because he was going to work afterward. A lot of people would probably be going to work afterward, or else, wherever they usually went. Later, there was a football game at school and a hop. If it stopped raining, everybody would probably go to the game and hop like they usually did. So nothing had changed.

I kept staring out the window, watching the rain, and the cars, and the people with their umbrellas, and the collars of their overcoats pulled up. Thinking how nothing had changed, but everything had changed. I knew it would never be the same again.

I would have to find a way to be brave.

CHAPTER THIRTY

After the brief graveside ceremony, of which I remember nothing, save for the hard, cold, pelting rain and ripping wind, we gathered back at Big Jim and Pauline's house, in a small, cloistered group of close friends and family. A few tortured souls huddled over casserole dishes and drinks, in desperation of some semblance of normalcy, caught in an unimaginable circumstance.

Among us who returned to the house were several of Jimmy's closest friends. Pauline called them, along with me, into his bedroom. She asked us to choose whatever we wanted of his personal belongings. His closet was thrown open. His normally neat desktop was full, his bed piled high, everything pulled out from everywhere. My eyes fell on various objects—his bowling ball in its carrying case, unzipped, by his desk, bowling shoes, a jacket I knew he favored askew on a hanger in the closet bereft of its owner.

I was stupefied, bewildered, unable to grasp what it was I was being asked to do. I walked out uncomprehending—taking nothing. Pauline then shut the door, and no one entered the room again. It was as though the door was plastered over from that time forward until the house was eventually sold and demolished.

From the date of his passing, as it later appeared in our high school yearbook—In Memoriam, November 2, 1960, "Not lost, but gone before"—sweet sixteen arrived swiftly. The December birthday cake, with the make-a-wish candles, and then the winter 'Snowball Prom' followed—with the Cinderella dress and ruby slippers I wore to dance the night away with my high school dreamboat football star boyfriend.

At the end of that sophomore year, I left my high school to attend an academy of beauty culture in the city—never to graduate with my classmates. Thus began my odyssey to leave it all behind: the childhood, the memories, the life I had once imagined. The bond with the one person I was most tethered to had been broken.

I fled, went to college, and worked in another state, married, divorced, moved for more college in another state. Crisscrossed the country as though I had gypsy in my blood instead of unrelinquished grief in my soul.

As time went on, I visited less. Home was where I happened to be at the moment. I stayed in constant touch with those dear, but not often near. Family emergencies through the years, plane descending through the clouds, airport in view—heart full of dread, a foil for the sorrow.

I was not the only one. All of us closely tied to Jimmy, through birthright or love, were looking for an escape. What I had once felt, right after the funeral, that life would never be the same actually came to pass, in my family, and in Jimmy's.

EPILOGUE

U pon hearing my once childhood voice, and then with the writing of my memoir, the journey, in which I eventually came to understand what I had done, began. And to finally admit my "failure to thrive" marriage to an amicable divorce, to face the reality of the deep, abiding friendship that it was, not the intimate love relationship it appeared to be. And to pursue wholeheartedly what I felt had always been my true calling— my writing. But equally as important, it set me on a course to face my terror from the past, my deeply embedded grief and pain.

As did I, Jimmy had a younger sister who was four years old when he died. Strangely enough, our mothers were pregnant at the same time and gave birth a few months apart. Mary was Jimmy's younger sister, and Rose Marie was mine. Their births had come after the casino had closed, and my parents had bought the restaurant a few blocks away, and we moved, which is why they weren't included in the book. Although, they were another cord that drew our families together, kept them together, and that tightened the bond that much more for Jimmy and me.

They were born to a different set of circumstances than we were, most specifically my sister, Rose Marie, as she never spent her early years, as Mary did, in the once casino house by the railroad tracks, but they became close friends. The night Jimmy was killed, Rose was having a sleepover with Mary at Jimmy's house. They were kindergarteners when it happened. The girls provided great solace for our parents, no doubt, especially our mothers.

Many years later, right after my mother died and I was about to enter my forties, I spoke with Pauline on the phone. For the first time since Jimmy's passing, I brought him up. In all those years, we had spoken of many things, but never talked of his death. I asked her what happened to the numerous pictures of Jimmy and me that I knew she once took. I had heard she burned them. She said she didn't, but she gave them away. She put them in a small trunk and gave them to friends. She said she couldn't bear to keep them. They have never been found—as though they never existed, like our lives together never happened.

Pauline said the pain was too great, and she had to go on. She had to raise Mary. Our mothers, by their natures, were better able to carry forth. Our fathers had a more difficult time.

They floundered.

Big Jim, more so, early on from the loss of his only son; my father, as he aged. They became ranters and ravers. Both were astute, intellectual men who could not reconcile their consciences with man's inability to be moral versus an innate desire of self-interest and, often, greed.

My father and I had many discussions on the subject when I was in college, as first, a psychology/sociology major, and then a law major. All the while, taking writing courses as electives, dreaming of a writing career, and then, in a different direction, involving myself in design and art. Conflicted as usual! In those early years after Jimmy's death, I was torn between doing the practical and logical as Jimmy would have done and my own riskier inclinations based on some unknown faith of good outcomes.

In our talks, my dad would go back to those years when they operated the casino, as though he were stuck in that period of his life. He was unable to let go of the anger he felt as to how people could so easily turn a blind eye to wrongdoing, or find themselves trapped in it as he and Big Jim had been, unable to run a legal casino, but given a wink and a nod, protected by the powers of a crooked government system. He hated the corruption and hypocrisy in what he had seen and still saw all around him.

He was very fixated on how power was doled out to those who had the money and means to acquire positions of authority. If they were devious, they could use the law to their advantage, especially when it came to vice. Creating laws against alcohol, gambling, and such created a situation for the unscrupulous to game the system, including those on both sides of the law. He was adamant that vices couldn't be stopped, only controlled by laws to punish those who participated and harmed others through their engagement.

When my father and Big Jim had the casino, numerous ones were operating all over the city—illegal gambling halls in the back of restaurants, sports centers, bars, and private golf and bowling clubs. As my father said, it was a big business that "greased a lot of palms," particularly those who were sworn to uphold the law, not use it for their own gain. He said it made a mockery of all we stood for as a country.

He felt operating illegally had been forced upon him and Big Jim. He got worse after a stroke in his later years and railed, relentlessly, against those in positions of political power and authority—certain they were up to no good if even a hint of such arose. He had seen too much of what power could do in the wrong hands.

Big Jim died of cancer, only eight years after Jimmy died when Mary was but twelve. The big house where Jimmy, Mary, and I spent our young years was sold to a discount store and torn down. Pauline and Mary moved into a townhouse. Pauline took a job clerking for a local store, and my mother soon followed, working together and remaining best friends all their lives until my mother's death. Mary had moved away to attend college as I had, and stayed in a faraway city to work after graduating. After my mother's passing, when Pauline retired, she followed to be with Mary. Not long after, Pauline passed away also.

Then, everyone lost touch with Mary as she married and moved again. Unbeknownst to each other, both of us becoming vagabonds, escaping from a lost time and the pain of it. Neither of us returning to the place of our birth. It would be many years until we reunited. It would take a book on illegal gambling casinos and social media to bring us together. And this memoir that you are reading, that Mary spent hours line editing, to help us bond as sisters again, not of the flesh, but of the heart.

When we finally connected, I also reconnected with others I hadn't seen or heard from since I was a teenager—all the high school classmates of Jimmy's and mine. I was to discover many missing pieces that I had never understood as classmates had avoided the subject of Jimmy's death around me. I was to learn that because of our father's casino and the unscrupulous characters that illegal elements attracted, there had been talk back then by someone on the police force that Jimmy had been murdered as a vendetta against Big Jim. Another friend told me he had thought that also—that Jimmy was incredibly agile as a runner and bowling champion to have just slipped under the train, something was fishy, he would think that for eternity. The story was that Jimmy was followed after his card game and was thrown under the wheels. When he died, I had such a hard time imagining that he would have jumped a train after what had happened to us as children that I had never told anyone. No proof ever surfaced, so we will never know.

The reconnections I made occurred by chance, or so it seemed. However, I will always wonder if it was by chance or some psychic phenomenon as those reconnections happened just as I was finishing the memoir, bringing more to light. Along with that uncanny twist of fate, another piece of information surfaced. It came from one of Jimmy's card gaming buddies, Lester. Lester had been one of Jimmy's closest friends. It was at his house where they had been playing cards the night Jimmy died, which I had known, but vanquished from my thoughts—frozen in time by the only thing that mattered. Jimmy, gone.

On a whim, after several email conversations, I told Lester about the memoir and asked him if he would like to read it. He said yes. Mary was editing it and emailed him a copy.

Afterward, he told me how he had lived with a pain in his heart all the many years since, feeling somewhat responsible over Jimmy's death, and how Jimmy had come to have to walk home that cold November night.

It was Lester's mother who was to drive Jimmy home.

But it seems she had a drinking problem, and Jimmy realized she had had one too many. Lester told me, Jimmy—always polite, impeccably mannered, and dressed in street clothes—declined, made light of it, and said he'd run home, "Thanks anyway, Mrs. Bailly."

Lester said, " We went out the back door, and Jimmy knew I was feeling bad about my mom. I said I was sorry, and we locked eyes. Jimmy just laughed, brushed it off like it was no big deal. He said, 'See you tomorrow, Bailly!' Then he turned and was gone." Lester stopped, blinking back tears, then added, "The devastation of the following morning was unfathomable."

As it had also been for me—unfathomable. Lester said he had never really forgiven his mother for being drunk. He said, "I'm not sure that guys our age knew what love or deep friendship was, but Jimmy was a great source of my strength in life, and I have never been able to shake Jimmy's memory of that night, of Jimmy's steady gaze. Just like he always was, steady." Lester thanked me for sending him the manuscript, saying, "my soul needed Jimmy Dugan back inside of me."

With the writing of the book, reliving that time with Jimmy, the love we had for our families, and so many of those myriad adults that made up our youth, and above all, each other, I came to see what I had done to survive Jimmy's terrible death. I not only physically ran from where we were raised—I left emotionally. I found a way to be brave as we had always believed we needed to be as children to withstand the chaos we saw all around us.

There were good aspects that came out of that upbringing as I also ran from situations and people who might draw danger, or discord, like that which had plagued our parent's lives, and ours. From all I had heard, seen, and experienced with Jimmy at an early age, I was wise enough to recognize and flee from trouble and those who cause it.

Only, it wasn't bravery in the true sense of the word. It left a large part of my life as an adult woman barren of the bliss and richness that comes with the grownup intimacy of love. For the most part, I did not do it consciously, but to protect myself from a hurt that had hollowed out my heart.

After Jimmy's death, I developed a strong propensity for practicality when it came to grief and matters of sentimentality. I looked upon my romantic adventures with a jaundiced eye. I was often drawn to men who weren't good candidates for long-term commitments, and those who were, I chose for safety, sensing that closeness with them was not an achievable goal— for them or for me—as I feared intimacy, feared closeness.

I had never come to grips with Jimmy's death. Instead, I bolted, left the scene as fast as I could, created a sense of denial. I compartmentalized my life, leaving the past out along with what I had been unable to change and accept. I became a master at intellectualizing grief—refusing to sit with it—to give myself over to the deep sorrow I lived with, always shoving it back under the surface until it infested my being.

As the years came and went, I found myself drawn to those situations and people that had a comforting feel of familiarity. Only, from time to time, I often felt dispossessed and lonely. I never felt quite at home anywhere—a misfit. There were emotions I covered up very well that only materialized in the obscure stories I often wrote or in quickly dashed-off poetry scribbled and tucked away in books, stuffed in drawers, lost and forgotten. Time passed, events came and went: high school over, popular girl, smiling, smiling, and laughing—an easy escape for a buoyant personality loving life. Years rolled on, away to college in a far-off state where I was to remain, an honor student once my painful dyslexia was better managed and hidden like my shameful upbringing—overachieving, pretty, silly girl full of fun, though a more serious demeanor often camouflaged by charm and design.

There were those bumps in the road, the *man thing*, and marriage, trying to circumvent life's necessary conventions with a minimum of emotional involvement. Not as difficult as it proved, I was to discover. Many men were taking the same road, dodging intimacy and perhaps as afraid of the dark, the stillness—as afraid of what true closeness might expose or bring, some also running from something. As afraid of pain as I was—

mine, a certain fear of screams that had once come in the night to tell of incomprehensible horror and heartbreak.

More time passed, businesses built, much money made, friendships formed, beautiful people, lavish black tie and ball-gown parties, sunny days; but midnight hours often until dawn always writing, squeezing out time to peck at typewriter keys like a bird out on a limb in frigid winter scouring for that very last dried up berry, hurting with hunger, searching for honest and sincere sustenance to fill me, under the veneer of the precarious safety I had formed on a rickety labyrinth paved with outer glory.

My victorious lifestyle in a modern city was vastly differ-ent, unrecognizable, from that of my origins. In my mid-thirties, I was a respectable, socially prominent career woman residing in a well-appointed vintage mansion I had recently finished renovating, after months working with a team, and as a designer, doing most of the artistic work myself. My Frank Lloyd Wright style house was on a Southern boulevard where other stately homes stood with their long manicured lawns, fountains, and statuary, while flowering shrubbery of pastel petals fluttered in the breeze, as swaying weeping willows rustled through the air.

I had worked through college, juggling jobs and school, gone quickly into entrepreneurship with a marital partner that allowed my creative skills to shine. He, with a natural affinity for facts and figures, and I, with organizational skills as a writer and visual artist, made a good team. We first built an empire of a company together. Rising stars, we created an active social life. Then we split our talents to a more desirable degree, with him running the company, while we bought and refurbished a vintage home with me at the helm. Swiftly, after selling it, we bought the much larger, massive one I completed. These were huge undertakings and the main glue that had been holding us together, but like an old repaired chair that had held too much weight, that glue had started to crack and buckle. The thought had crossed my mind, *what now, what next, how big the project, the Taj Mahal Hall?*

I had accomplished all that I ever dreamt of through the lens of practicality. I was a calculated visionary. No rose-colored glasses for me. Those had been ripped away years before when Jimmy died. Realism was my specialty. Any endeavor was viewed for its advantages and disadvantages. Particularly, in matters of the heart. No luxury of sentimentality did I allow myself.

On the surface, my life was an overwhelming success—save for a void I had begun to realize that had never been filled. One that I had hidden even from myself. It was certainly not in my relationship that masqueraded as the perfect marriage, but functioned more like the corporation it was—a union spewing out material wealth and lots of sparkly surface glitter, but lacking any real depth other than that of commerce.

I had the fairytale fantasy I had longed for during all that unsettled and trauma-laden childhood, but once my life slowed down with the big renovation project finished, I started feeling a great deal of sadness. There was barrenness in my spirit and an emptiness in my soul. I had finally achieved what I had strived so hard to obtain—but I sensed what was most important, most precious, was missing. Lost.

My husband and I had created a facade of love in a lifestyle surrounded by beauty and success, lending itself to a vision of marital happiness. But, what we left out between us was any authentic depth of genuine emotion, the kind that wells up from the soul of one's being, encompassing the full range of all human feeling, exposing vulnerability and fear. We had refused to do so, caught up in the creation of an illusion.

To deeply love is to expose ourselves to risk. It calls upon us to recognize primordial pain that wails in the night for what can be lost that cannot be replaced. Those human souls that we bond with, that once gone, we can only cry for, bereft without them, for days, months, years, however long it takes to accept their parting, we that have been left behind, forced to go on without them.

What is paramount in order to live in an abundance of spirit, to find true happiness, I was to learn, you must have the willingness to let go of the pain from your past. In our fast-paced, modern lives, we tend to move on quickly, especially the younger we are, as I was when Jimmy died. I was longing for bright and sunny days, rejecting and refusing the gloom of grief. Only, running from grief is running from the reality of earthly life itself, as just as there is summer, winter will come. Flowers bloom and grace us with their loveliness, and then they die. Pain and loss are just as much part of life as is joy and plea-sure. Grief eventually comes to us all. Grief doesn't dissipate on its own accord, as I tried to make it do by ignoring it as though it doesn't exist.

I had refused to acknowledge it and call it to the surface. I had not allowed myself the honesty of what I was avoiding. I tried to evade truth with a fantasy story like I had used as a child to repel sadness.

I clung.

I was not willing to let go. Perhaps, by a sense of loyalty, or a sense I could keep Jimmy with me, drag the past along, emotionally make time stand still. Fear and pain corrode. It blinded me to the truth of the moment. Until that fateful day at the railroad crossing with the whistle blasting and blasting, as though to force me to face all that I had been running from, especially the situation at hand; my fake and barren marriage of any true intimacy and closeness like I had once known.

When Jimmy passed away, I had not been willing to stand

CAROLINE SHANNON DAVENPORT

in grief's presence. I had not been willing to weep into the night, to give myself over to the cleansing sorrow of it, and the acceptance of what was out of my control. I had not been willing to face that I would have to live the rest of my seemingly forever life without the one person who was my compass, my navigational and trusted guide into a world I found confusing and often filled with dishonesty.

As children, we were both struggling to find a way to navigate an adult world we didn't understand. We used different means as we aged. They worked for us then, still young, not yet adults. What would Jimmy have chosen had he lived? And me? Would I have followed him, challenged him?

I was the one left to ponder.

Many references have been made about an unexamined life not being worth living. I believe it is because unexamined we are always tied, trapped in our past, for most of us, trapped in childhood, trapped in whatever long ago situations we might have been born into, or damaged from, unwilling to see or acknowledge.

Whatever early or later life events force us into dark places, if we refuse to bring them into the light of awareness, they can never be released. My greatest hope in this novelistic memoir is that others will find the courage to open their Pandora's Box and uncover their avoidances that have cobbled their own lives. I now know through experience once I let go and began to live in a space unoccupied by hidden anguish, a light came forth to fill my days. The beauty of the here and now, shined, not smudged and tainted by my longings of yesterdays.

I have often wondered what Jimmy would have done if he had lived, set on a course for ferreting out only the facts—the seeable, believable reality—just as I was set on a path of overindulgence for fractured fantasies. Both of us were, then, too young to grasp that the answers might lie someplace closer to the center, where, unencumbered by the past, the view would be clearer and the truth evident. I would like to think it would be even expansive enough for Jimmy to walk with me, take my hand, and believe—as he once had—in magic.

Without the magic all that I had attained had not been enough. Safe and secure, years of hard work behind me, always barreling forward at breakneck speed, rushing from project to project, there was always in the background of my conscious-ness, like the barely perceptible dinner music at some fine French restaurant, a soft, relentless refrain of that whistle signaling the ongoing freight train that was my well-concealed, emotionally unsettled life. And my sense of awareness at just how unsettled it was, had daily become apparent to me when I encountered the train at the railroad crossing and was gripped by the terror I felt at its shrill sound.

ACKNOWLEDGMENTS

There are no words strong enough to encapsulate my overflowing heart full of all the love and gratitude I feel for the generosity, kindness, and encouragement given to me over the years enabling me to sustain a belief in bringing this book forth. Without family and friends alike I would have floundered. There were cliffs to climb in my writing career from early on, and with time forward, when my legendary agent and mentor, Clyde Taylor of Curtis Brown, Ltd, met a too early demise, and when sorrow and an unforeseen illness claimed my publishing desires. Soldiering on with more practical, achievable, endeavors, but always with stories stealing into my thoughts. And characters making their way, with pen on pad, late into nights or early morn during the periods when the fog of my malady lifted, until fate provided a miraculous cure. Clear of mind and full of energy to find my way down onto the rocky shore where so many others would, like lifeboats, come to lead me to the promised land with their suggestions, their insight, their fine skills. To all of them I list, my thank you's are boundless.

Teri Donahue who read the first manuscript, and taught me how to operate, type it into a word processor, Walter Rabchuk, for his schooled editing, and concise reasoning, and both of them for their immense friendship in those early days and onward. Mary Ann Dugan, sister of the heart, for her editing, technical knowledge, and hours spent verifying memories and her unwavering faith. David Parmer, John Mauk, Paula Champagne, David Eastburn for their fine editing suggestions that enlightened my own visions with clarity, Gail McAleer for her computer skills and time given freely with so much help, as Lyza Luke gave, with her hours retyping parts of the original manuscript. And Terry Shaffer whose research and book, *Illegal Gambling Clubs Of Toledo*, was so valuable. And JoAnn Flanagan, as historian in the county of origin with her accuracy of time and place, photos and newspaper clippings, articles, all bolstered my recollections. Then there are the readers, the many who read with open minds, and provided me with their feelings and thoughts. They gave me ideas and courage to move forward: Donna Brant Wess, Clare Wheeler-Brandt Hurst, Victoria Ford, Joanna Mclaren, Mary Hipp, Becky Breeden Buehrer, Wendy French, Kim Bourgea, Tom Wolfson, sisters by love: Sharon Moylan, Ellen Mary Forte, Diane McCutcheon, Jennifer O'Donnell. Hardly least but most, whose editing, computer knowledge, steadfastness, and deep devotion put the final manuscript over the finish line, my dear and loving husband, Kenton Scott "Skip" Bell.

Finally, with deep appreciation Running Wild Press and Lisa Kastner, the publisher, CEO of the company and the numerous talented artistic, production staff who brought this book you hold out of the darkness and into the light of day. And with special consideration to my talented, brilliant, kind, and forgiving editor, Benjamin B. White.

Running Wild Press publishes stories that cross genres with great stories and writing. RIZE publishes great genre stories written by people of color and by authors who identify with other marginalized groups. Our team consists of:

Lisa Diane Kastner, Founder and Executive Editor
Cody Sisco, Acquisitions Editor, RIZE
Benjamin White, Acquisition Editor, Running Wild
Peter A. Wright, Acquisition Editor, Running Wild
Resa Alboher, Editor
Angela Andrews, Editor
Sandra Bush, Editor
Ashley Crantas, Editor
Rebecca Dimyan, Editor
Abigail Efird, Editor
Aimee Hardy, Editor
Henry L. Herz, Editor
Cecilia Kennedy, Editor
Barbara Lockwood, Editor
Scott Schultz, Editor

Evangeline Estropia, Product Manager
Kimberly Ligutan, Product Manager
Lara Macaione, Marketing Director
Joelle Mitchell, Licensing and Strategy Lead
Pulp Art Studios, Cover Design
Standout Books, Interior Design
Polgarus Studios, Interior Design

Learn more about us and our stories at www. runningwildpress.com

Loved this story and want more? Follow us at www.runningwildpress.com, www.facebook.com/runningwildpress, on Twitter @lisadkastner @RunWildBooks